HOW TO NAME YOUR BUSINESS IN THE UNITED STATES

Find and Protect the Name of Your Company in the USA and Abroad

VINCENT ALLARD

CorpoMax

Publisher
CorpoMax Publishing LLC

Cover Design
Marie-Andrée Lemieux - malem.com

Cover Image
© alexlmx - 123rf.com

ISBN
E-book ISBN: 978-1-952012-10-5
Paperback ISBN: 978-1-952012-04-4

Edition
First Edition

Series
Second book in the YES TO ENTREPRENEURS® series

WHAT THEY SAY

"Simple. Clear. Precise. Complete. Reading Vincent Allard is having a great time, with a friend who gives us, without pontificating, the best advice to help us succeed in setting up a business in the USA. Cartesian, he divides the challenge into three parts, three books, to properly analyze, explain and better solve difficulties. A must."

Richard JOHNSON, Retired Journalist, Journal of Montreal

"Books such as those in the *Yes to Entrepreneurs* series provide businesses with useful information and practical tools to expand into the United States market, the largest consumer market and recipient of foreign direct investment in the world."

Gina BENTO, Commercial Specialist, U.S. Department of Commerce, International Trade Administration

"Never before have guides been so deserving of the term *practical*! With his trilogy, Vincent Allard offers us in a controlled, organized, complete, but also airy and digestible way everything there is to know about setting up a business in the United States, its name and its banking management. I keep these books on my desk, within easy reach. That is how useful they are."

Bernard GEENEN, Economic and Commercial Counselor, Wallonia Export & Investment Agency, Consulate of Belgium, New York

"I received and read carefully the three guides by Vincent Allard, lawyer and founder of CorpoMax. I am delighted because it is an undeniable help for any entrepreneur who wants to start a business in the United States. It's simple, you are guided and you can feel Vincent Allard's great experience through his advice and recommendations. Also for the legal practitioner, it is a source to many questions that our French and European clients ask us. Congratulations again and thank you!"

Isabelle LANDREAU, Lawyer of the Paris Bar, Founder of Smart Law Fabrik

"My business is advising emerging Canadian companies on developing their business in the United States. I have been doing that for a long time. The aspects of incorporation, setting up bank accounts, even choice of name for doing business in the U.S. can seem complicated. But these guides are great. Everything you need to do is spelled out simply and directly, requirement by requirement, issue by issue. They are ideal for entrepreneurs looking to do business in the United States. Easy to read and to the point. Everything basic that is involved is clearly laid out. I highly recommend their use."

Tom CREARY, Managing Director of WestbridgeOne Consulting, Founder and Past Chairman of the American Chamber of Commerce in Canada - Quebec Chapter

"The *Yes to Entrepreneurs* book series is extremely structured, complete and easy to use, like the services offered by CorpoMax. This solid and valuable work greatly simplifies the task of entrepreneurs, advisers and lawyers. It adds value to our advice and makes the American dream very accessible. We wish this collection a long life and thank Vincent Allard for his permanent dedication."

Serge BOUGANIM, Lawyer of the Paris and Brussels Bars

"Finally a practical and clear guide to answer the questions that any entrepreneur wishing to create a business in the United States is asking !!! The success of an establishment depends above all on good knowledge of the rules of law but also of local commercial practices. In this respect, the corporate name of the company is crucial and the practical advice given by Mr. Allard in his work is particularly relevant and useful. In general, the three books published by Mr. Allard provide a better understanding of the legal issues related to setting up a business in the United States and will help entrepreneurs in carrying out their project."

François BOSCHER, Lawyer of the Tours Bar (1981-1992) and the Quebec Bar (1995- ...), Former President of the French Chamber of Commerce and Industry in Canada - CCIFC

"Congratulations to my colleague Vincent Allard for the publication of three exceptional popularization books for entrepreneurs who want to start a business in the United States. Reference books, advice books, more than 600 pages that guide us in the land of Uncle Sam to get the best results."

Pierre CHAGNON, Retired Emeritus Attorney, Bâtonnier of Quebec

"As someone new to American business, there is so much information, on-line, consultants, advisors, it's all very intimidating. Tell it to me straight... and at last we have it! In easy and amusing terms that gave me confidence in making the right choice, to start my business in America."

Captain Peter FABIAN (ret.), CEO, Advanced Coatings Engineering LLC

"A master at simplifying complex information for all to understand, Vincent Allard has succeeded in putting together a concise, well written and easy to read series on starting a business in the United States. The *Yes to Entrepreneurs* series takes you by the hand and guides you through the steps of incorporating a company, naming it appropriately and even starting a bank account. This series is full of practical information and a must read for both legal professionals looking to gain knowledge in basic American corporate legal issues, and for the motivated entrepreneurs looking to get one step closer to living the American dream."

George VARDATSIKOS, Ph.D.(med.), LL.L., Attorney of the Quebec Bar

"This series of practical guides allows entrepreneurs and professionals who advise them to benefit from the experience of thousands of other entrepreneurs who have started their business in the United States. There are a lot of details that could help their own business."

Robert CHAYER, U.S. Tax Expert, Canada

"Reading highly recommended. Three essential and very comprehensive guides for all immigrant candidates who wish to familiarize themselves with the important concepts to start their professional installation in the United States. These books are very well structured and expose in a very instructive way, but in a simple and accessible language, the concepts to know to make informed decisions concerning their American structure. From the corporate form to the choice of name, including tax implications, everything is there."

Estelle BERENBAUM, Immigration Lawyer, Florida

"Creating companies and doing business in the United States is a journey full of pitfalls. As a European, we underestimate the complexity of American law and its implications. Vincent Allard's Yes to Entrepreneurs collection provides ready-to-use pragmatic knowledge to successfully navigate American *waters*."

Arnaud LABOSSIÈRE, CEO, The Free Minds Press Ltd

"The information contained in Mr. Allard's trilogy of books will be extremely useful to any entrepreneur wishing to enter the U.S. market. The high quality of information is presented in a structured manner and is easily accessible, due to the author's great talent in simplifying complex matters."

Patric BESNER, Besner Business Lawyers

CONTENTS

4 - TYPES OF BUSINESS NAMES

5 - HOW TO CHOOSE YOUR BUSINESS NAME

6 - HOW TO PROTECT YOUR BUSINESS NAME

7 - HOW TO CHANGE YOUR BUSINESS NAME

8 - CONCLUSION

EXCLUSIVE BONUS

Throughout the process of writing this guide, I accumulated many hyperlinks that greatly enrich its content.

An up-to-date list of these hyperlinks can be found at the web address listed in the *Useful Resources* section, at the end of this guide.

DEDICATION

I dedicate this practical guide to all entrepreneurs who want to find the best name for their future company. I hope this guide will stimulate their inspiration.

1 - INTRODUCTION

1.1 - PRESENTATION

Welcome to this practical guide on how to name your business in the United States.

My name is Vincent Allard. I am a business lawyer, but first and foremost, an entrepreneur who moved to the United States in 1999. For nearly 20 years, through my website corpomax.com, I have helped thousands of entrepreneurs from more than 50 countries start their businesses in the United States.

OBJECTIVES

This practical guide is mainly intended for you, an entrepreneur who wants to find a name for his or her future company.

However, this guide can just as well help you find a name for your business in any other country, as long as you pay attention to the local laws.

This guide has two objectives.

. . .

Objective no. 1 is to make sure you fully understand the essential features your business name must have, in simple and clear language.

Objective no. 2 is to provide you with the necessary tools to choose and protect your business name.

IMPORTANT DECISION

Choosing a business name is one of the first and most important decisions you will make as a business owner. Choosing a name for your business is just as crucial as choosing good employees and suppliers. Over time, the name of your business will undoubtedly become one of its most important assets.

Your business name will be important:

- To your customers, whose initial contact with your business will most likely be its name, whether they hear it or read it
- To your employees, who will be responsible for communicating this name to all the persons they deal with in their daily activities
- To your suppliers, who will want to be able to easily identify your business
- To your competitors, for whom you will want to become a benchmark of quality, so as to differentiate yourself from them
- To you, as the founder of a business you want to proudly lead to the very top.

POINTS TO CONSIDER

Here are five points to consider:

1. First, all of the rules we are going to analyze are important.
2. Second, any rule can have an exception.
3. Third, these rules apply not only in the United States, but also in any other country, subject to local laws.

4. Fourth, the remarks that follow can sometimes apply not only to the business name, but also to a trade name or trademark.
5. Finally, there is no perfect guide for naming your business. It is a creative process based on an inexact science.

PRACTICAL GUIDE

Attention! This practical guide is not a legal, accounting, or tax guide. For this, you will need to consult professionals working in these areas.

This guide is essentially practical and contains many examples:

- Examples of business names, trade names, trademarks, and domain names
- Examples of current names and names of the past
- Examples of names on the *Fortune 500*® list
- Examples in English and French

In short, this practical guide has been prepared for easy reading and immediate understanding.

I sincerely hope this guide will provide you with the information and inspiration you need to choose the best name for your business.

If you have any questions, comments, or suggestions regarding this practical guide, including its *Useful Resources* section, feel free to contact me.

Thank you and good reading!

1.2 - IMPORTANT DEFINITIONS

From a legal point of view, there are different types of names. However, from a practical point of view, the line between them is often blurry. Here are some definitions to help you understand them better.

CORPORATE NAME

A corporate name is the company's official name, as it appears in its articles of incorporation:

- Amazon.com, Inc.
- Apple Inc.
- CorpoMax Inc.
- Google LLC
- Microsoft Corporation

The corporate name is used only to identify the company from a legal point of view. Therefore, it does not play an advertising role as such.

TRADE NAME / BUSINESS NAME

A trade name - also known as a business name - is the name under which the business is operated and known by the general public. It may or may not be identical to the company's corporate name:

- Amazon
- Apple
- CorpoMax
- Google
- Microsoft

FIRM NAME

A firm name is the name of a partnership. It often consists of the names of the partners. Historically, the majority of professionals do business together in partnership:

- Accountants
- Architects
- Engineers
- Lawyers
- Etc.

For example, when I was practicing law, my partner Richard Pigeon and I were doing business together as *Pigeon, Allard, Attorneys at Law*. However, professionals are increasingly being given the right to do business through a corporation.

ASSUMED NAME

An assumed name is the trade name under which a company does business and which differs from its legal name. For example, the company ABC Inc. does business under the assumed name *Gogopro*. In the

United States, assumed names are called by different names, depending on the state or popular language:

- Assumed Name
- Business Name
- DBA Name — DBA for *Doing Business as…*
- Fictitious Name
- Trade Name

TRADEMARK

A trademark is a sign that distinguishes the products or services offered by a business. The following are the main types of trademarks:

- A word mark: the word NIKE
- A design mark: the Nike swoosh, without any words
- A word and design mark: the word NIKE with the swoosh

A word mark can often be identical to the corporate name - without the legal identifier - or to the trade name of your company.

DOMAIN NAME

A domain name is a word or series of characters, followed by a specific extension, which identifies a specific computer within a network of interconnected computers. In everyday language, a domain name is a specific address on the Internet. The following are the main types of domain names:

- Generic: amazon.com
- Geographical: paypal.fr
- Sector-based or descriptive: mcdonald.restaurant

Finally, here are three points you should remember.

1. RULES

The rules we are going to analyze generally apply to corporate names just as well as trade names — and sometimes even trademarks.

2. SPECIALIZED LAWYER

These rules do not replace the advice of a lawyer or legal counsel working in your jurisdiction, who specializes in corporate or intellectual property law. For any questions that apply to your particular situation, I strongly encourage you to consult such a specialist.

3. ADVERTISING

It is rare for a company to use its corporate name in its advertising. Instead, it uses its trade name or trademark.

2 - CHARACTERISTICS OF THE BUSINESS NAME

2.1 - LENGTH OF THE NAME

Your business name must be short.

ADVANTAGES OF A SHORT NAME

There are many advantages to a short name.

For your customers, a short name is:

- Easy to hear
- Easy to remember
- Easy to read
- Easy to pronounce
- Easy to write
- Easy to share

For your employees and yourself, a short name is:

- Easy to communicate to your customers and suppliers

For your graphic designer, a short name is:

- Easy to incorporate into your logo, website, and printed materials

DISADVANTAGES OF A LONG NAME

There are also many disadvantages to a long name:

- Difficult memorization by your customers and suppliers
- Overly long domain name
- Overly long email addresses
- Name often distorted or shortened
- Name often transformed into abbreviation or acronym

TODAY

Modern companies adopt short names:

- Amazon
- Apple
- eBay
- Google
- PayPal

Many traditional companies shorten their name:

- American Broadcasting Corporation > ABC
- American Family Life Insurance Company > Aflac
- America Online > AOL
- American Telephone and Telegraph Corporation > AT&T
- Applied Molecular Genetics > Amgen
- Banque Nationale de Paris > BNP
- British Petroleum > BP
- Consumer Value Stores > CVS

- Dairy Queen > DQ
- Federal Express > FedEx
- General Electric > GE
- Hewlett Packard > HP
- International Business Machines > IBM
- Kentucky Fried Chicken > KFC
- Minnesota Mining and Manufacturing Company > 3M
- Royal Bank of Canada > RBC
- The Wall Street Journal > WSJ
- Turner Broadcast System > TBS
- Union Bank of Switzerland > UBS
- United Parcel Service > UPS
- Weight Watchers > WW

Finally, here are three points you should remember.

1. IDEAL WORLD

In an ideal world, your business name should consist of:

- Ten characters or less
- One or two syllables, three at most
- One word, or two at most

2. ACTIVITIES

It is recommended not to include a description of your company's activities in its name:

- CorpoMax U.S. Business Incorporation Inc. vs. CorpoMax Inc.

3. FORTUNE 500®

From among the 20 largest U.S. businesses on the Fortune 500® list:

- 45% have a name composed of only one word
- 50% have a name composed of two words
- 25% have a name composed of only two syllables
- 15% have a name composed of three syllables.

2.2 - SPELLING OF THE NAME

Your business name must be easy to write.

It is important that the name be written the way it sounds:

- Without the need to provide an explanation
- Without the need to spell it

If not, your customers and suppliers will often make spelling errors when writing to you.

TO AVOID

To prevent your business name from constantly being distorted, you should avoid:

Adding letters

- Dig > Digg
- Fiver > Fiverr

Deleting letters

- Flicker > Flickr
- Tumbler > Tumblr

Replacing letters

- News > Newz
- Photo > Foto / Fotto
- Reserve > Rezerve

Using a phonetic shortcut

- Easy > EZ / Ezi
- Energy > NRJ
- Experience > Xperience
- Explorer > Xplorer
- Express > Xpress
- Extra > Xtra

Combining letters and numbers

- For You > 4U
- Illuminate > Illumin8
- Motivate > Motiv8

Using abbreviations

- International > Intl
- Marketing > Mktg

~

Here are four risks you run if your business name has an odd spelling:

1. Your potential customers will not find your business on the Internet, because they will not remember the spelling change.

2. Your potential customers will confuse your business with another one whose name is spelled in a more traditional way.

3. People will not be able to recommend your business to contacts, friends, and family members because they will not remember how to spell its name.

4. If your company name is heard - on the radio, for example - people will naturally write it with the usual spelling.

Finally, here are three points you should remember.

1. NATURAL WAY

Name your business in the most natural way. So your potential customers will remember the spelling of the name, not the change in its spelling.

2. LISTEN

Close your eyes and say the name of your business. If you hear a word from the dictionary, it should be written as in the dictionary. In addition, verbally ask your friends and relatives to write the name you have chosen. If more than 50% of them are mistaken in writing it, there is a problem.

3. FOREVER

If you distort the spelling of a common word, your employees and yourself will have to spell it forever.

2.3 - PRONUNCIATION OF THE NAME

Your business name should be easy to pronounce.

EASY PRONUNCIATION

In fact, it should be easy for everyone to pronounce:

- Your employees
- Your customers - both current and potential
- Your suppliers
- Your banker
- The media
- Yourself

Your business name should also consider:

- The language of your customers
- The target market for your business

Easy pronunciation results in easy writing and easy memorization.

According to an American study published in 2006 by two researchers at Princeton University, a stock symbol or company name that is easy to pronounce can be an important factor in short-term price increases.

Now, here are five problems relating to the pronunciation of your business name:

1. IDENTICAL PRONUNCIATION OF TWO DIFFERENT WORDS

- Birth - Berth
- J - Jay
- Mail - Male

2. DIFFERENT PRONUNCIATION OF TWO IDENTICAL WORDS

- Lead
- Live
- Resume

3. DIFFICULT PRONUNCIATION

- WSFS Bank

4. UNKNOWN PRONUNCIATION

- Oneok: Is this word pronounced O-nay-oak or One-okay? The Wikipedia online encyclopedia tells us how to pronounce the name of this American public company. This proves that there is an obvious problem of pronunciation.

5. HEARING CONFUSION BETWEEN TWO LETTERS

- B - P
- F - S
- M - N

Finally, here are three points you should remember.

1. LANGUAGES

The pronunciation of your business name should be easy in all languages:

- Amazon
- Apple
- Coca-Cola
- Microsoft
- Toyota

A free tool to check the pronunciation of your business name in various languages is *Google Translate* by clicking on the *Listen* icon.

2. HOW TO PRONOUNCE

If you have to tell people how to pronounce the name of your company, change your name right away! Your ultimate goal is simple: avoid people constantly asking you to repeat your business name.

3. CONFUSION

The pronunciation of the name should not be confused with another word.

Before choosing the name *Amazon*, Jeff Bezos chose *Cadabra* - as in *Abracadabra.* However, when Jeff pronounced *Cadabra* in front of his lawyer, he thought he heard *Cadaver.* Bezos quickly chose another name, now known around the world.

2.4 - SOUND OF THE NAME

Your business name must have a pleasant sound.

A pleasant-sounding name is easier to memorize.

The sound of your business name has a musical dimension that should not be underestimated. It can sometimes even lead to a sense of energy and excitement in the minds of your potential customers.

RHYMES AND ALLITERATIONS

According to various studies, exposure to a business name or trademark that has a repetitive phonetic structure can have a positive effect in the minds of consumers, both in terms of memorization and recall.

In fact, rhymes and alliterations can fix a name in people's minds and make it easier to remember.

A rhyme is when two words have an identical final sound:

- Coca-Cola
- Hubba Bubba
- Jelly Belly
- LexisNexis
- Tutti Frutti

An alliteration is when two words begin with the same letter:

- Best Buy
- Bits & Bites
- BlackBerry
- Coca-Cola
- Constant Contact
- Dunkin' Donuts
- Jimmy John's
- Kit Kat
- Krispy Kreme
- LifeLock
- PayPal

LANGUAGE AND CLIENTELE

The sound of your business name should be nice in all languages, or at least in the languages used in the markets you are targeting.

In addition, the sound of the name must be analyzed according to the targeted clientele.

Some words convey predominantly feminine values, such as words ending with the letter *a*:

- Activia
- Sephora
- Veolia

Other words convey predominantly masculine values, such as words ending with the letter *o*:

- Gringo
- Nintendo

Finally, here are three points you should remember.

1. EYES CLOSED

Close your eyes and say your business name aloud. If you like its sound, that is a good sign.

2. WRITTEN VS. ORAL

A name can be interesting in writing, but much less orally. In such a case, forget it!

3. DIFFERENT SOUND

Do you want your business to be different from its competitors? If so, choose a different sound.

2.5 - VISUAL ASPECT OF THE NAME

Your business name must be visually pleasant.

It is important to visualize your business name in several places:

- On your business card
- On your stationery
- On your website
- In your domain name
- In your logo
- In your advertising
- In your promotional materials
- On your billboard

Some business names or trademarks are visually well balanced.

Some names consist of letters with round shapes:

- GOGO

Others names do not contain any low letters:

- VOLVO

Finally, some names display a symmetry between the first and the last letter:

- XEROX
- OREO

Finally, here are three points you should remember.

1. LOWERCASE AND UPPERCASE

Analyze the visual aspect of your business name in upper and lower case. Are you satisfied with the result?

When I launched CorpoMax in 2001, I wanted this name to be visually pleasing regardless of how it was written:

- CorpoMax
- Corpomax
- corpomax
- CORPOMAX

2. DOMAIN NAME

What will your business name look like in its domain name, especially if it has two or more words?

- expertsexchange.com: Experts Exchange or Expert Sex Change?
- penisland.net: Pen Island or Penis Land?

To avoid any confusion, it is sometimes better to capitalize the first letter of each word:

- ExpertsExchange.com
- PenIsland.net

Another solution, although not recommended, is to insert a hyphen between the words of the domain name:

- experts-exchange.com
- pen-island.net

3. SHORT NAME

Keep in mind: the shorter the name of your business, the more pleasant its visual aspect will be.

2.6 - MEANING OF THE NAME

Your business name must have a meaning.

This name must mean something or at least create an impression with people who will see it or hear it for the first time.

Therefore, it can be:

- Intriguing
- Mysterious
- Positive
- Reassuring
- Surprising
- Etc.

Ideally, your business name should create a positive first impression.

POSITIVE CONNOTATION

Here are some business names with a positive connotation:

- BestBuy
- BrightHouse
- SunTrust

Words related to the family are often popular:

- Baby
- Children
- Family
- Mom & Pop
- Sons & Daughters

The same goes for words related to physical and mental health:

- Happiness
- Health
- Life

WORDS TO AVOID

On the other hand, there are some words you should not use in your business name.

Avoid words with a negative connotation. Nevertheless, some of these words have been used successfully:

- The Boring Company — founded by Elon Musk, creator of the Tesla automobile
- Poison — perfume
- Fossil - watches
- Superdrug — stores selling beauty products

Avoid words that make people think of other words:

- Analtech
- Master Bait and Tackle

Avoid words that have a negative or obscene meaning in a foreign language. For example, in 1999, automobile manufacturer Mazda introduced a pickup truck named *Laputa*. However, the word *puta* means *prostitute* in Spanish and Portuguese. Under pressure from its dealers, Mazda had to rename its vehicle for these specific markets.

Finally, here are three points you should remember.

1. PLANET

Always check the international implications of the chosen name. Because of globalization and the Internet, your potential market is usually the entire planet. Know the meaning of your business name around the world in order to avoid nasty surprises.

2. A STORY, PLEASE!

People love stories. So, tell a story. After choosing your business name, prepare a web page explaining the origin of this name.

3. TARGET MARKET

Choose a name that matches and is understood by your target market.

2.7 - ORIGINALITY OF THE NAME

Your business name must be original.

Original means:

- Attractive
- Memorable
- Unique

The name must not mean anything to anyone. A bland name is not a good idea.

COMPETITION

Your business name should differentiate itself from the name of your competitors.

- If not, your company will blend in with the bulk of your competitors.
- If not, your customers may confuse your business with your competitors.

According to some studies, nearly 90% of U.S. companies choose a name similar to that of their competitors. This is particularly true in the field of aviation, which favors geographical reference:

- American Airlines
- Alaska Airlines
- Hawaiian Airlines
- Northwest Airlines
- Southwest Airlines

However, newcomers have changed this:

- Allegiant Airlines
- JetBlue Airways
- Virgin Airlines

ORIGINAL NAMES

Some original names managed to stand out quickly:

- Banana Republic
- GoDaddy
- Indeed
- Monster
- The Body Shop
- Yahoo!

VERBS

If your business name has the potential to become a verb in popular language, it is even better.

- Dropbox
- FedEx
- Google

- Twitter
- Xerox

Finally, here are three points you should remember.

1. SECONDS

Your business name only has a few seconds to make a good impression.

2. DO NOT COPY!

Never copy the name of your future competitors, even if they have not taken any steps to protect it legally.

3. LONG TERM

Think long-term. Will the name you choose today still be as original in five or ten years?

3 - ELEMENTS OF THE BUSINESS NAME

3.1 - BEGINNING AND END

TOP OF THE ALPHABET (A, B, C)

Since always, it is recommended to choose a business name whose first letter is at the very top of the alphabet:

- Amazon
- Apple
- AT&T

This was particularly true in the past, when companies were listed alphabetically in phone books.

But still today, some algorithms and directories create lists based on alphabetical order.

Often at trade shows, exhibitions, trade fairs, and other professional events, exhibitors are presented in alphabetical order:

- In the visitor's guide
- In the list of exhibitors
- On the event website

A critic, commentator, or journalist who analyzes various companies will often list them on an alphabetical basis.

BOTTOM OF THE ALPHABET (X, Y, Z)

For their part, business names with the first letter at the bottom of the alphabet are often at a disadvantage, especially when it comes to:

- Their position in directories
- Their pronunciation, which is often more difficult

Of course, there are some exceptions, mostly from a huge marketing budget:

- Xerox
- Yahoo!
- Zillow

EMPTY WORDS

Avoid inserting an empty word in your business name.

An empty word is a word with no special meaning and only has a grammatical purpose:

- The Home Depot
- The UPS Store

DISADVANTAGES OF EMPTY WORDS

In general, empty words:

- Perpetuate an old way of naming a business
- Do not add any value to your business name
- Needlessly lengthen this name

- Make it more difficult for your customers to memorize the name.

The first letters of your business name are among the most important for memorization and recall purposes. Why replace them with empty words?

EMPTY WORDS AND DIRECTORIES

Empty words also cause problems in directories.

Some directories leave the name intact:

- The UPS Store

Other directories move the empty word to the end of the name, preceded by a comma:

- UPS Store, The

Finally, some directories simply remove the empty word:

- UPS Store

So the mere inclusion of an empty word results in three different versions of your business name. This is obviously not recommended. For its part, the U.S. Internal Revenue Service (IRS) systematically omits any empty word when it issues the EIN - Employer Identification Number - in favor of a company:

- Company Name: The Grand Canyon Adventures Inc.
- EIN number issued to: Grand Canyon Adventures Inc

EMPTY WORDS AND DOMAIN NAMES

Empty words often force companies to reserve at least two domain names:

The Home Depot

- thehomedepot.com
- homedepot.com

The North Face

- thenorthface.com
- northface.com

The UPS Store

- theupsstore.com
- upsstore.com

The Wall Street Journal

- thewallstreetjournal.com
- wallstreetjournal.com

Finally, here are three points you should remember.

1. AMAZON

One of the reasons Jeff Bezos, the founder of Amazon, chose this name is because he wanted it to appear at the top of the directories.

2. FACEBOOK

An empty word is generally useless. Mark Zuckerberg quickly realized it after launching *thefacebook.com* in 2004. Shortly after, he paid $200,000 to acquire the rights to the domain name *facebook.com* and send the empty word *the* into oblivion. However, he permanently redirected the old domain name towards the new one.

3. EXCLUSIVE OR REPEATED

The inclusion of an empty word can make sense - especially for a brand - when the focus is on the empty word itself, to emphasize a notion of exclusivity:

- THE Travel Specialist

In addition, repeating an empty word can sometimes be worthwhile:

- The Beauty and the Beast

3.2 - SINGULAR AND PLURAL

In some situations, it may be wise to have a business name that is plural:

- AMC Theatres
- XYZ Laboratories

Some words can be used in singular or plural, without any real difference:

- Family Holding vs. Family Holdings
- Total Enterprise vs. Total Enterprises

In many U.S. states, the availability of a company name is checked on the basis of an identical spelling. Therefore, if the name you have chosen is already used by someone else, you can consider its plural version:

- Family Holding vs. Family Holdings

The situation is the same with regard to domain names. If the domain name you have chosen is already used by another person, nothing prevents you from using its plural version:

- FamilyHolding.com vs. FamilyHoldings.com

Finally, here are three points you should remember.

1. NETWORK

Some words used in the plural immediately give the image of a network and not of a single person, establishment, or service:

- Allard & Partners
- Best Caribbean Travels
- Hilton Hotels

2. CONFUSION

Beware of the risk of confusion! If your company is a holding company without any real contact with consumers, the risk of confusion is lower than if you are actively working with the public.

3. ORIGINAL

If the desired name is not available, be original and do not use its plural form. Choose another name instead. Otherwise, there will be a high likelihood of confusion when your potential customers try to find your website and end up with another company.

3.3 - NUMBERS

There are various ways to use one or more numbers in your business name. Here are some examples:

- 7-Eleven
- Motel 6
- Super 8

TELEPHONE NUMBER

Some companies use numbers in their advertising, especially to help consumers retain their toll-free number - *numéro vert* or green number in Europe:

- 1-800-GO-FEDEX
- 1-800-Got-Junk?

POPULARITY OF A1

In the United States, the term *A1* is often used in popular language because it means *perfect, excellent, really good.*

- This car is in A1 condition.

Three versions are generally used:

- A and 1 glued together: A1 Towing
- A and 1 separated by a hyphen: A-1 Garage
- A and 1 each followed by a period: A.1. Steak Sauce

NUMBER AT THE BEGINNING OF THE NAME

Sometimes the number is at the beginning of business names.

Here are some examples:

1st Choice

- Your business name will be among the first in the directories.
- However, your customers will not know how to write it. On the phone, they will hear and then write *First Choice*, in letters only.
- What will your domain name be: 1stchoice.com - with the number 1 - or firstchoice.com - all in letters?
- What happens if one of the two domain names is not available? This will confuse the minds of your potential customers.

2G

- Your customers will not know how to write it: *2G* - with the number 2 - or *Two G* - with the word *two*?
- In addition, spaces are generally not mentioned orally, thus creating a permanent risk of error.

NUMBER AT THE END OF THE NAME

Sometimes the number is at the end of business names. Here are some examples:

Illumin8

- Visually, this name is original.
- However, your customers will not know how to write it. On the phone, they will hear and then write *Illuminate* - with the letters *A-T-E* instead of the number *8*.
- In writing, your foreign customers will not know how to pronounce it. A French customer may think your business name is pronounced *IlluminHuit*.

NUMBER SIMILAR TO A LETTER

Sometimes it can be tempting to replace a letter with a number that looks like it. Here are some examples:

G00gle

- It can sometimes be interesting from a graphic point of view.
- However, this creates typographical confusion in the minds of your customers.
- How will they write the name of your company?
- Imagine you spell your business name…
- How are you going to spell its domain name?

Cartel

- In writing, the risk of confusion can sometimes be high, depending on the nature and size of the font used.

V1ctory

- In writing, the risk of confusion may be just as great, for the same reasons.

CONFUSION BETWEEN NUMBER AND LETTER

In some cases, there may be real confusion between a number and a letter.

Is X a letter or number? It all depends...

Since the launch of the iPhone in 2007, Apple had always used an Arabic numeral to identify different versions of its models:

- iPhone 5, iPhone 6, iPhone 7, etc.

In 2017, Apple launched a new iPhone, going from a sequence of Arabic numerals to a Roman numeral, without any warning.

As a result:

- Half of the planet pronounced the letter X for iPhone X.
- The other half pronounced the number 10 for iPhone 10.

Business naming experts believe that using numbers in a company name is rarely a good idea. When numbers are associated with letters, the name of a company is harder to memorize and harder to recall.

Finally, here are three points you should remember.

1. POTENTIAL CUSTOMERS

Always think of your potential customers when you tell them the name of your company:

- What will they hear?
- What will they remember?
- What will they write?
- What will they look for?

2. MEANING

In some countries, a number may have a special meaning. For example, for Chinese people:

- The number *4* means bad news.
- The number *6* represents luck.
- The number *7* is like their word, which means vital energy.
- The number *8* represents wealth and money.

3. FORTUNE 500®

In the Fortune 500® directory, only four companies have one or more numbers in their name:

- 3M
- Group 1 Automotive
- L3 Technologies
- Phillips 66

In addition, only six companies have a number written in letters in their name:

- Capital One Financial
- Fifth Third Bancorp
- First Data
- FirstEnergy
- First American Financial
- Twenty-First Century Fox

3.4 - LOWERCASE AND UPPERCASE

When a company is established in the United States, the register of the state in which it was created generally indicates the company name in uppercase letters only. However, the company is free to display its name in any format it prefers:

- All letters in uppercase: CORPOMAX INC.
- All letters in lowercase: corpomax inc.
- First letters in uppercase: Corpomax Inc.
- Some letters in uppercase: CorpoMax Inc.

INSERTED UPPERCASE LETTERS

Several companies insert uppercase letters in their name, especially when it consists of two words or parts of words:

- BestBuy
- BlackBerry
- CorpoMax
- FedEx
- LinkedIn
- PayPal
- YouTube

The use of uppercase letters can often distinguish words or sequences of words in the name of your company:

- BetterRates vs. Betterrates

LOWERCASE AT THE BEGINNING

Other companies prefer having their business name or product name start with a lowercase letter:

- eBay
- iPhone
- lynda.com
- salesforce
- udemy

~

But as a rule, follow the example of the vast majority of companies born before yours: choose to put the first letter of the name in uppercase.

This will save you from having to repeat tirelessly - and needlessly - to your customers, partners, and suppliers, that the first letter of your business name is lowercase.

Anyway, 99% of them will always indicate an uppercase letter at the beginning of the name of your company.

Finally, here are three points you should remember.

1. NAME VERSIONS

Always compare the different versions of your business name, in several fonts:

- All in uppercase letters
- All in lowercase letters
- First letter of the name in uppercase
- First letter of each word — stuck together or not - in uppercase

2. CONFUSION

Beware of the risk of typographical confusion!

- Uppercase letter *I* vs. lowercase letter *l* — depending on the font

3. DOMAIN NAME AND EMAIL ADDRESS

Nothing prevents you from using uppercase letters in your domain name and email address:

- www.CorpoMax.com
- info@CorpoMax.com

3.5 - PUNCTUATION AND TYPOGRAPHIC SIGNS

PUNCTUATION SIGNS

In English language, the main punctuation marks are:

- Period .
- Comma ,
- Semicolon ;
- Question mark ?
- Exclamation mark !
- Colon :
- Ellipsis ...
- Parentheses - sometimes referred to as brackets ( )
- Square brackets [ ]
- Quotation marks “ ”
- Hyphen –
- Forward slash /

TYPOGRAPHIC SIGNS

Still in English, the main typographic signs are:

- Braces - sometimes referred to as curly brackets { }
- Apostrophe ‘
- Asterisk *
- Chevrons - sometimes referred to as pointy brackets < >
- Ampersand &
- Tilde ~

INTERNAL REVENUE SERVICE – IRS

The Internal Revenue Service — IRS — which handles taxes in the United States, retains no punctuation marks when issuing your company EIN number.

For example, your company name is:

- INTER-ALIAS CHARLIE’S, INC.

The IRS will extract any punctuation and typography, to retain only:

- INTER ALIAS CHARLIES INC

DIRECTORIES

For their part, the directories act in various ways. Take for example the name A.B.C. Garage.

The first directory will keep the punctuation marks.

- A.B.C. Garage

The second directory will omit punctuation marks without removing spaces.

- A B C Garage

The third directory will omit punctuation marks and spaces.

- ABC Garage

The advantages of using punctuation or typographic signs in your company name are almost non-existent.

The only advantage is probably to attract attention, at least temporarily:

- Yahoo!

However, this can sometimes be wise for trademarks:

- Guess? Jeans
- 1-800-Go-FedEx
- 1-800-Got-Junk?

This last example is interesting in several ways:

- Telephone

The phone number provides a direct link to the company.

- 1-800

1-800 immediately tells people that it is a toll-free number in North America.

- Two Words

The words *Got* and *Junk* indicate what the company does, in addition to completing the phone number.

- Question Mark

Finally, the question mark confirms a simple question to potential customers: *Do you have garbage that you want to get rid of?*

~

However, the disadvantages of inserting a punctuation or typography into your company name are numerous. Let us analyze some of them.

PERIOD

Strangely, the period is still popular in the name of a company. However, it often causes more problems than it solves. Here are some examples.

A.D.S.

- Orally, how are you going to say the name of your company? *A period D period S period*?
- How will your customers, suppliers, or contacts find your company in search engines?
- How will they write the name of your company in their contacts, records, or databases?
- How will they guess your domain name?

INC.

- Generally, there will be a period at the end of the short version of a corporate identifier: *Inc.* for *Incorporated, Corp.* for *Corporation.*

U.S.

- In theory, the rule is to separate these two initials with periods.
- In practice, some use periods, others do not.

USA

- As a general rule, there is no period between these letters.

EXCLAMATION MARK

The exclamation mark became popular with Yahoo!

This punctuation mark offers an image of energy and excitement.

Note that Yahoo! is the only well-known company to use an exclamation mark in its business name.

HYPHEN OR DASH

The hyphen is often used as a strong link between two partners or legal entities - following a merger, for example.

It is generally not recommended to use a hyphen in your company name:

- When you communicate the name of your company, are you going to say *hyphen* or *dash* between the words?
- Some of your customers will include the hyphen, others will not, resulting in two versions of your business name.
- You will need to reserve two domain names to make it easier for potential customers to search your business on the Internet: cocacola.com and coca-cola.com.

AMPERSAND

At the graphic level, the ampersand is interesting. But its use in the name of your company is not recommended.

Paul & Jane

- Orally, how are you going to say the name of your company?
- How will your customers, suppliers, and contacts find your company in search engines?
- How will they guess your domain name?
- How will they write it: with or without space?

To date, a domain name cannot contain an ampersand. This must be replaced by the word *and* or the contraction *n*, which adds two different versions of your company name.

APOSTROPHE

The apostrophe is used in at least three circumstances.

It is part of a person's name:

- O'Reilly Auto Repairs

It indicates possession:

- McDonald's — at *McDonald*

It indicates the omission of one or more letters in a contraction:

- Park 'N Fly — *Park and Fly*

COMMA

The comma is sometimes used in the name of an American company:

- Bodson, Taylor and Kraft

It is also sometimes used to separate the name from its legal identifier:

- Cocorico, Inc.

PARENTHESES OR BRACKETS

Parentheses are sometimes used in the name of a company to identify a subsidiary:

- Random Industries (USA)

They are also sometimes used to indicate a year of foundation, to distinguish a new company from a previous one:

- Random Industries (2020)

In the latter case, adding the year in the new company name creates a real distinction in the minds of customers and creditors of the previous company.

But the oral problem remains. Are you going to always tell your customers and suppliers: "*Random Industries open parenthesis 2020 close parenthesis*"?

In addition, some states, including New Jersey, refuse to create companies whose names include parentheses.

Finally, here are three points you should remember.

1. REFUSAL

A U.S. state may refuse the name you submit for your new company because of punctuation or typography marks.

Therefore, the name of your company should contain only:

- Letters from the Latin alphabet - a, b, c ...
- Arabic numerals - 1, 2, 3 ...
- Roman numerals - I, II, III ...

2. GOOGLE! AND MICRO-SOFT

From October 1998 to May 1999, Google was known as *Google!* - with an exclamation mark. But this punctuation sign was quickly removed and never came back, which was a good decision.

For their part, Bill Gates and Paul Allen began doing business together under the name *Micro-Soft*, before eliminating the hyphen and joining the two words.

3. FORTUNE 500®

In the Fortune 500® directory, the name of 13 companies contain an ampersand, eight with spaces and five without spaces:

- American Axle & Manufacturing
- Bed Bath & Beyond
- Goodyear Tire & Rubber
- Johnson & Johnson
- March & McLennan
- Owen & Minor
- Procter & Gamble
- Stanley Black & Decker
- AT&T
- BB&T Corp.

- M&T Bank Corp.
- PG&E Corp.
- S&P Global

Nine companies have an apostrophe in their name:

- Casey's General Stores
- Dick's Sporting Goods
- Lowe's
- Macy's
- McDonald's
- Kohl's
- Land O'Lakes
- O'Reilly Automotive
- Peter Kiewit Sons'

Ten companies have a period in their name:

- Arthur J. Gallagher
- C.H. Robinson Worldwide
- D.R. Horton
- J.B. Hunt Transport Services
- J.C. Penney
- J.M. Smukers
- R.R. Donnelley & Sons
- W.R. Berkley
- W.W. Grainger
- U.S. Bancorp

Twelve companies have a hyphen in their name:

- A-Mark Precious Metals
- Auto-Owners Insurance
- Bristol-Myers Squibb
- Colgate-Palmolive

- Core-Mark Holding
- Freeport-McMoRan
- Harley-Davidson
- Kimberly-Clark
- Owens-Illinois
- Parker-Hannifin
- Sherwin-Williams
- Twenty-First Century Fox

Only one company has a name bearing quotation marks:

- Toys “R” Us

This shows that 91% of the 500 largest U.S. companies have no punctuation or typographic signs in their name.

3.6 - ACCENTED CHARACTERS

FRENCH LANGUAGE

In French, there are mainly fourteen accented characters:

- à â
- ç
- é è ê ë
- ï î
- ô
- ù û ü
- ÿ

SPANISH LANGUAGE

In Spanish, there are at least seven accented characters:

- á
- é
- í
- ñ

- ó
- ú ü

REALITY

In the United States, despite the fact that the Spanish language is increasingly used, English still reigns as king and master. In addition, there are no accented characters in Shakespeare's language.

Not only do U.S. state computer systems not accept accented characters, American computer keyboards do not contain any.

In addition, domain names do not contain accents.

In short, you cannot use accented characters in the name of your American company, at least for now.

Finally, here are three points you should remember.

1. TRADEMARKS

Unlike company names, some trademarks for products and services offered in the United States have accents. These brands, with a foreign sound, attract the eye, the ear, and therefore the attention of potential customers:

- Estée Lauder
- Häagen-Dazs
- L'Oréal
- Pokémon

2. HESITATION

The presence of an accented character could lead to hesitation in the pronunciation of your company name. Indeed, Americans are not used to seeing accented characters. But, on the other hand, it could offer an interesting element of differentiation. Anyway, for the moment at least, it is not possible.

3. FORTUNE 500®

No name of the 500 companies in the Fortune 500® directory contain accented characters.

3.7 - SPECIAL CHARACTERS AND MATHEMATICAL SIGNS

SPECIAL CHARACTERS

In American English, the main special characters are:

@ : The at sign - or *at symbol* or *commercial at*

: The number sign - or *pound sign* or *hashtag*

$: The dollar sign

MATHEMATICAL SIGNS

The main mathematical signs are:

+ : The addition sign - or *plus sign*

- : The subtraction sign - or *hyphen-minus* or *minus sign*

x : The multiplication sign - or *times sign* or *dimension sign*

÷ : The division sign - or *obelus*

% : The percent sign

ADVANTAGES

The only advantage of using a special character or mathematical sign in your company name is potentially at the graphic level.

DISADVANTAGES

However, there are many disadvantages. Here are some examples:

Etic@

- Always the same problem when speaking: how will you communicate the name of your company?
- How will your potential customers find your company in search engines?
- A name containing the at sign may be refused by the state in which you want to create your American company.
- As of today, the at sign cannot be used in a domain name.
- By choosing the domain name *etica.com*, your business name will be used in two different ways. Remember the fundamental rule: always use and display the name in the same way.

Coroweb +

- Orally, how will you say the name of your company? Will you explain each time that the word PLUS is not really a word, but rather the mathematical plus sign?
- How will your customers, suppliers, and business contacts find your company in search engines: Coroweb +, Coroweb+, Coroweb Plus, CorowebPlus?
- How will they guess your domain name: coroweb+.com, corowebplus.com, coroweb-plus.com?

Note that a mathematical sign cannot be used in a domain name, except the minus sign, which is also a hyphen or dash.

Finally, here are three points you should remember.

1. NOT RECOMMENDED

It is absolutely not recommended to use special characters or mathematical signs in your company name.

Always ask yourself the same four questions:

- How will you verbally communicate the name of your company?
- How will your potential customers hear it?
- How will they write it, without you having to spell it out?
- How will they search for your company on the Internet?

2. ORIGINAL NAME

Find an original name and not an original way to write it. Do not confuse the name of your company with its graphic representation in an advertisement.

3. FORTUNE 500®

No company names in the Fortune 500® directory contain special characters or mathematical signs, except for the hyphen or dash between some words.

3.8 - REPEATED CHARACTERS

There are several ways to use repeated characters in the name of your company. Here are some examples:

REPEATED CHARACTERS, STUCK TOGETHER IN THE WORD

- Booz Allen Hamilton
- Exxon
- Google
- Molson Coors Brewing
- Wanadoo
- Yahoo!

REPEATED CHARACTERS, NOT STUCK TOGETHER IN THE WORD

- Clorox
- CorpoMax
- Costco
- Microsoft

REPEATED CHARACTERS, AT THE BEGINNING OF THE WORD

- Mmmuffins

REPEATED CHARACTERS, AT THE BEGINNING OF SEVERAL WORDS – ALLITERATION –, STUCK TOGETHER OR NOT

- Bed Bath & Beyond
- Best Buy
- BlackBerry
- Coca-Cola
- Constant Contact
- Dunkin' Donuts
- Krispy Kreme
- LifeLock
- PayPal

REPEATED CHARACTERS, AT THE END OF THE WORD

- Fiverr
- Qualcomm

REPEATED CHARACTERS, AT THE ENDS OF THE WORD

- Oreo
- Xerox

Finally, here are three points you should remember.

1. DOUBLE O

The most popular repeated characters — stuck together — are the double O:

- Google

The most popular repetitions are the vowels a, e, i, o, and u:

- Bazaar
- Buutchiis
- Feever
- Yahoo!

For their part, repeated consonants are found in several common words in the dictionary:

- Apple

2. SOUND

The repetition of characters can sometimes be interesting in terms of sound, which is appreciated by the human brain:

- Xerox

3. FORTUNE 500®

In the Fortune 500® directory, among the names with a repetition of characters other than dictionary words, the most popular are:

- Google
- Exxon Mobil

3.9 - REPEATED WORDS

Some company names consist of identical or similar words. This repetition of words can sometimes be interesting.

IDENTICAL WORDS

- CamelCamelCamel
- Johnson & Johnson
- Pillow Pillow
- PizzaPizza

SIMILAR WORDS

- Coca-Cola
- Jelly Belly
- PayPal

Finally, here are three points you should remember.

1. DISTINCTIVE NOTE

Repetition sometimes adds an interesting distinctive note. Moreover, just as you have experienced in the past with your parents and teachers, repetition promotes memorization.

2. DOMAIN NAME

In some cases, word repetition may be useful if the domain name for the chosen name is not available:

- pizzapizza.com

3. FORTUNE 500®

In the Fortune 500® directory, there is only one company whose name is made up of repeated words, at least in terms of sound:

- NRJ Energy

3.10 - WORDS STUCK TOGETHER

The trend for words glued together started at about the same time as the popularity of the Internet. Indeed, since there is no space between the words in a domain name, the eye and the brain have become accustomed to seeing glued words:

- Facebook
- GameStop
- Kickstarter
- MasterCard
- PayPal
- PulteGroup
- Skillshare
- Snapchat
- YouTube

Sticking two words together in a company name can sometimes lead to an unexpected result, especially in the domain name:

- penisland.net = Pen Island dot net or Penis Land dot net?

MERGERS AND ACQUISITIONS

When two companies merge together, it often happens that the name of the company resulting from the merger contains the two old names.

Sometimes, the two names are stuck together:

- AmerisourceBergen
- BorgWarner
- ConocoPhillips
- DowDuPont

Sometimes, the two names are separated by a hyphen:

- Colgate-Palmolive
- Freeport-McMoRan
- Bristol-Myers Squibb

But generally, there is a space between the two names:

- Berkshire Hathaway
- JPMorgan Chase
- Kraft Heinz
- Lockheed Martin
- Molson Coors Brewing
- Stanley Black & Decker
- Time Warner

Finally, here are three points you should remember.

1. "THEY ARE STUCK TOGETHER"

At the beginning, you will have to say to your stakeholders: *The words are stuck together*. Will this only happen at the beginning?

2. UPPERCASE

It may be advantageous to capitalize the beginning of each stuck word, making it easier for the eye to read and for the brain to remember:

- PenIsland

3. GRAPHIC DESIGN

Graphic design can make a big difference, precisely to facilitate memorization.

3.11 - INITIALISMS AND ACRONYMS

INITIALISM

An initialism is a series of letters which are the initials of a series of words, and which are pronounced individually:

- CNN: Cable News Network
- HP: Hewlett Packard
- UPS: United Parcel Service

ACRONYM

An acronym is an initialism that is pronounced like an ordinary word:

- AIDS: Acquired Immune Deficiency Syndrome
- FIAT: Fabbrica Italiana Automobili Torino
- GEICO: Government Employees Insurance Company

POPULARITY

Some company or brand names, consisting of initialisms or acronyms, are very popular. They are generally supported by a large marketing budget.

- BP: British Petroleum
- BMW: Bayerische Motoren Werke
- DHL: Dalsey, Hillblom and Lynn
- HSBC: Hongkong and Shanghai Banking Corp.
- IBM: International Business Machines

ADVANTAGES

The advantages of using an initialism or acronym in your company name are rare, but interesting.

- First, the name is short.
- Second, the name is usually easy to pronounce, especially when vowels and consonants are used together.

DISADVANTAGES

The disadvantages are more numerous.

1. The name can lead to a high risk of confusion.

Confusion can be audible, especially on the phone.

- B - P
- F - S
- M - N

Confusion can be visual, especially for dyslexic people.

- DVB - DBV

Confusion can be real, with existing initialisms or acronyms, in the United States or elsewhere in the world. For example, the initials GRC may mean:

- Governance, Risk Management and Compliance Management
- Gibson Research Corporation
- Gendarmerie Royale du Canada

2. The name may be difficult to pronounce.

- WSFS Bank

3. The name may have a negative meaning in another language.

- FTW: These initials have no particular meaning in French but can refer to the naughty expression *F..ck the World* in English.

UNWANTED INITIALISM OR ACRONYM

If your company name is made up of several words, it can lead your customers, employees, and suppliers to transform this name into an initialism or acronym that may not make you happy:

- International Software Integrated Systems > ISIS
- Data Analytics Enterprise Systems Host > DAESH

IN SHORT

Almost unanimously, experts recommend not to use initialisms or acronyms in the name of your company:

- It will not mean anything to anyone but yourself.
- Its distinctiveness will generally be low.
- Its memorization will be low, unlike invented or common words.

- This is a perfect route to anonymity.

In addition, since the initialisms and acronyms are made up of a limited number of letters, the corresponding domain names are generally no longer available.

Finally, here are three points you should remember.

1. EY

When the accounting firm Ernst & Young decided to shorten its name by adopting EY, it was probably unaware that this initialism was also that of an adult magazine.

2. PERIODS OR SPACES

If you choose an initialism or acronym, it is preferable not to put a period or space between the letters:

- CAT instead of C.A.T. or C A T

3. MEMORY

To help memorize, indicate the words corresponding to the letters, under or near your company name, in all your written communications — website, business cards, invoices, emails, etc.

3.12 - LEGAL IDENTIFIER

The name of any legal entity doing business in the United States must have a suffix, known as a legal identifier.

This suffix indicates to third parties the legal form in which the company was created.

This legal identifier can have various names:

- Corporate ending
- Corporate suffix
- Company suffix
- Ending suffix
- Legal ending
- Legal suffix

DELAWARE

In the State of Delaware —the best place in the United States to create a company— the main legal identifiers vary according to the type of legal entity.

. . .

For a **For-Profit Corporation**, it will be:

- Association or Assoc.
- Company, Co or Co.
- Corporation, Corp or Corp.
- Incorporated, Inc or Inc.
- Limited, Ltd or Ltd.

For a **Non-Profit Corporation**, it will be:

- Club
- Foundation
- Fund
- Institute
- Society
- Syndicate
- Union

For a **Professional Corporation**, it will be:

- Professional Corporation, PC or P.C.

For a **Public Benefit Corporation**, it will be:

- Public Benefit Corporation or PBC

For a **Limited Liability Company**, it will be:

- Limited Liability Company, LLC or L.L.C.

AUTHORIZATION REQUIRED

The use of certain legal identifiers may require prior authorization from regulatory bodies:

- Bank
- College
- Credit Union
- Trust
- University

SPECIFIC ASPECTS

Now, here are some specific aspects to consider.

First, the legal identifier may or may not be preceded by a comma:

- CorpoMax Inc.
- CorpoMax, Inc.

Second, the legal identifier does not have to be located at the end of the name:

- CorpoMax of America Inc.
- CorpoMax Inc. of America

Finally, the legal identifier may be in an abbreviated or extended form:

- CorpoMax Inc.
- CorpoMax Incorporated

Finally, here are three points you should remember.

1. LEGAL NAME OR BUSINESS NAME

Do not confuse the legal name with the business name of your company. For example, if your trucking company is called *Fastway*

Corp., it will usually indicate *Fastway* on its trailers and not the full legal name - unless required by law.

2. SHORT VERSION

The short version of the legal identifier is much more popular than its long version. Do not forget the global trend to shorten company names.

- CorpoMax Incorporated vs. CorpoMax Inc.
- CorpoMax Corporation vs. CorpoMax Corp.
- CorpoMax Limited vs. CorpoMax Ltd

3. FIFTY STATES AND DISTRICT OF COLUMBIA

In the United States, there are 50 states - as well as the District of Columbia -, so 51 sets of specific rules regarding acceptable legal identifiers. What is allowed in one state is not necessarily allowed in another.

3.13 - LOGO

Although not part of the company's legal name, a logo often accompanies the business name. More importantly, the logo crystallizes and creates an important reminder in the minds of current and potential customers.

Over time, some logos identify the company, without even having to indicate its name:

- The Apple apple
- The McDonald's M
- The Nike *swoosh*

Some logos include the name of the company:

- The arrow under Amazon

It is more common for a company to change or replace its logo during the course of its existence than to change its name. Fashion, trends, and evolution mean that companies refine their logo on a regular basis, or even replace it with a new one, with no link to the previous one.

Finally, here are three points you should remember.

1. ENERGY

A beautiful logo will never fix a bad company name. So it is more important to focus your energy on choosing your company name rather than the logo that will be attached to it.

2. FAVICON

During the process of creating your logo, do not forget to include a favicon, a small icon that will be displayed in the browser's address bar when displaying the pages of your website.

3. NO NAME

It is often preferable to have a logo that does not include your company name, such as the McDonald's M or Apple fruit. Thus, the logo can exist by itself, without text, and be used in various ways.

3.14 - SLOGAN

According to the Merriam-Webster dictionary, a slogan is "a brief attention-getting phrase used in advertising or promotion".

SYNONYMS AND EQUIVALENTS

Here are some synonyms or equivalents of the slogan:

- Catchphrase
- Catchword
- Jingle
- Motto
- Strapline
- Tagline

TYPES OF SLOGANS

A slogan can help to locate a company in its business segment:

- De Beers - *A Diamond is Forever*
- Nikon - *At the heart of the image*

- Nokia - *Connecting People*
- U.S. Postal Service - *We deliver*

A slogan can contain only one word:

- 3M - *Innovation*
- IBM - *Think*

A slogan can contain two or three words only:

- Apple - *Think different*
- Garnier - *Take Care*
- Intel - *Intel Inside*
- LG - *Life is Good*
- Nike - *Just Do It*
- Subway - *Eat Fresh*
- Volvo - *For Life*

A slogan can have many words:

- FedEx - *When it absolutely positively has to be there overnight.*

A slogan can consist of two sentences or two series of words, separated by a period:

- Dollar Shave Club - *Shave Time. Shave Money.*
- Harley Davidson - *American by birth. Rebel by choice.*
- Kit-Kat - *Have a break. Have a Kit-Kat.*
- MasterCard - *There are some things money can't buy. For everything else there's MasterCard.*
- Smith Barney - *We make money the old-fashioned way. We earn it.*
- Walmart - *Save Money. Live Better.*

A slogan can be in uppercase and lowercase:

- L'Oréal Paris - *Because You're Worth It.*

A slogan can be in lowercase only:

- General Electric - *imagination at work*
- McDonald's - *i'm lovin' it*

A slogan can be in uppercase only:

- Marine Corps - *THE FEW. THE PROUD.*

A slogan may or may not have a period at the end:

- Dunkin Donuts - *America Runs on Dunkin'*
- Nike - *Just Do It.*

A slogan can be used by a company for a very long time:

- Avis - *We try harder (*50 years)
- De Beers - *A Diamond is Forever* (since 1948)

A slogan can play on words:

- Citibank - *The Citi never sleeps.*
- IBM - *I think, therefore IBM.*
- John Deere - *Nothing Runs Like A Deere*
- Red Lobster - *Sea Food Differently*

A slogan can contain a question:

- Allstate Insurance - *Are You in Good Hands?*
- CA Milk Processor Board - *Got Milk?*
- Capital One - *What's in your Wallet?*

- Clairol - *Does she or doesn't she?*
- Gatorade - *Is it in you?*
- UPS - *What Can Brown Do For You?*
- Verizon Wireless - *Can you hear me now?*
- Wendy's - *Where's the Beef?*
- Yahoo! - *Do you...Yahoo!?*

A slogan can distinguish the company from its competitors:

- Avis - *We try harder*
- BMW - *The Ultimate Driving Machine*
- Budweiser - *The king of beers*
- Chevrolet - *The Heartbeat of America*
- Disney - *The happiest place on earth.*
- Gillette - *The Best a Man Can Get*
- HSBC - *The World's Local Bank*
- Porsche - *There is no substitute Porsche*

A slogan can be in response to a competitor's slogan:

- IBM - *Think*
- Apple - *Think different*

IN SHORT

A slogan is not part of the company name, but becomes closely associated with it. It often complements and reinforces the company name in the public mind.To help keep your slogan in the minds of your current and potential customers, it should be used everywhere, such as:

- Website
- Email signature
- Correspondence
- Invoices

Finally, here are three points you should remember.

1. COCA-COLA

Coca-Cola has changed its slogan nearly 50 times since 1886. Here are some of them:

- 1969 - *It's the Real Thing*
- 1971 - *I'd like to Buy the World a Coke*
- 1979 - *Have a Coke and a Smile*
- 1982 - *Coke Is It!*
- 1985 - *America's Real Choice*
- 1986 - *Red, White & You*
- 1988 - *You Can't Beat the Feeling*
- 1989 - *Official Soft Drink of Summer*
- 1990 - *You Can't Beat the Real Thing*
- 1993 - *Always Coca-Cola*
- 2001 - *Life Tastes Good*
- 2003 - *Coca-Cola... Real*
- 2006 - *The Coke Side of Life*
- 2009 - *Open happiness*
- 2016 - *Taste the feeling*

* Source: coca-colacompany.com/stories/coke-lore-slogans

2. PROTECTION

U.S. intellectual property lawyers recommend protecting your trademarks, including your slogan. Famous companies — thanks in particular to their slogans! – regularly file trademarks with the United States Patent and Trademark Office — USPTO – to protect them. This clearly shows the importance these companies attach to their slogans:

- Apple: three trademarks for *Think different*
- Intel: seven trademarks for *Intel Inside*
- McDonald's: four trademarks for *i'm lovin' it*
- Nike: six trademarks for *Just Do It.*

If you want to adopt a slogan, first check if it is not already being used by another company. Prevention is better than cure....

3. NOT ESSENTIAL

Although interesting in some circumstances, a slogan is not essential. Like the logo, it is only one of the marketing tools at your disposal. Do not feel obliged to find one, especially at the beginning of your American adventure. Instead, focus your efforts on choosing the name of your company.

4 - TYPES OF BUSINESS NAMES

4.1 - NAME OF AN INDIVIDUAL

One of the oldest ways to name a company is to use the name of its founders. This method is still very popular among some service companies.

PROFESSIONAL SERVICES

- Accountants
- Architects
- Engineers
- Lawyers
- Psychologists

PERSONAL SERVICES

- Massage therapists
- Photographers
- Etc.

Generally, such a company name includes:

A FAMILY NAME

- Dell
- DuPont
- Ford
- McDonald's

TWO FAMILY NAMES

- Hewlett-Packard
- Goldman Sachs
- Procter & Gamble

A FULL NAME

- Estée Lauder Companies
- Philip Morris International
- Walt Disney

There are some advantages to using your name in your company's name.

EASY AND INEXPENSIVE SOLUTION

First of all, it is an easy solution, because the intellectual effort required to find the name is non-existent. In addition, this solution is less expensive because you do not use any external resources to help you - for example, a naming agency.

IMMEDIATE RECOGNITION

Second, this solution provides you with immediate recognition. It is ideal for instant recognition as a founder, manager, or important person in the company.

NOTORIETY OF THE FOUNDER

Third, this solution is interesting if you already have a significant reputation in a given field:

- Fender Guitars

MAIN FIGURE

Finally, it is generally advantageous to use the name of the main figure in the field of fashion, perfumery, and cosmetics:

- Coco Chanel
- Giorgio Armani
- Pierre Cardin
- Yves St-Laurent

However, there are many disadvantages.

TOO STRONG PERSONAL IDENTIFICATION

First, a company is less easy to sell when its reputation is intrinsically linked to the name of its founder.

DIFFICULT TO MEMORIZE

Second, using your name may increase the length of your company name.

When a business name is too long, customers will instead:

- Use only the first two names: Smith, Leary, Barney & Norman > Smith, Leary
- Create an initialism with the first letter of each name: Smith, Leary, Barney & Norman > SLBN

AGING OF THE NAME

Third, the name of the company is often linked to the aging of your own person, at least in the mind of people.

IMAGE PROBLEM

Fourth, the name of your company can sometimes give the impression that you are alone, if this name only includes yours.

CRIMINAL PROCEEDINGS

Fifth, if a member of your family is in the throes of criminal justice, the negative consequences, often fueled by traditional and social media, can damage your company's reputation.

AFTER-SALE PROBLEM

Sixth, if you sell the business that bears your name, and then want to use your own name in a different business venture, this may not be permitted under the sales agreement.

CHANGE OF COMPANY NAME

Finally, if there is a break between the founders of your company, or a withdrawal, addition, or death of a partner, changing your company name will sometimes have negative consequences, like:

- Significant costs
- Change of domain name
- New domain name not always available
- Unstable image among your customers

Finally, here are three points you should remember.

1. EXPERTS

Experts are almost unanimous: in general, it is not — or no longer — a good idea to use your name in your company's name.

2. SURNAME OR INITIALS

If you still want to do it, just take your last name or, better yet, your initials with another word.

This will make it easier for you to sell your business in the future, as it will not be clearly or solely identified with your own person:

- A & W Restaurants: Roy Allen and Frank Wright, founders
- Abbott Laboratories: Wallace C. Abbott, founder

3. FORTUNE 500®

In the Fortune 500® directory:

- More than 15% of company names contain a family name.
- More than 5% contain at least two surnames.
- More than 21% contain the names of their founders, either at the origin or by merger.

The majority of these companies were founded several decades ago, when it was common for them to bear the names of their founders.

4.2 - GEOGRAPHIC NAME

Some companies choose to use a geographic element in their name.

INTERNATIONAL GEOGRAPHIC ELEMENT

The insertion of an international geographic element in your company name can give it an image of grandeur, at least in the minds of your potential customers:

- Worldwide Accountants
- International Diamonds

This insertion can also be interesting if you want to take advantage of the reputation of a specific product or service in a particular place in the world:

- Belgium Waffles
- Dijon Mustard

NATIONAL GEOGRAPHIC ELEMENT

The insertion of a national geographic element can be judicious if you want to make a nationalist fiber vibrate:

- American Airlines
- Bank of America
- National Dentist Products

This insertion is often used to identify the American subsidiary of a foreign company:

- L'Oreal USA

REGIONAL GEOGRAPHIC ELEMENT

The inclusion of a regional geographic element is justified if it is the main region targeted by your company:

- Atlantic Insurance
- East Coast Pizza
- Pacific Cruises

However, to specify means to limit. Adopting a name with a regional geographic element can be detrimental if you later decide to expand your activities to other regions.

STATE GEOGRAPHIC ELEMENT

A state geographic element often refers to a characteristic or style specific to a state:

- California Pizza
- Kentucky Fried Chicken

The insertion of such a geographic element may make sense if several entities of the same group are located in various states, or if this is the market your company is targeting:

- ABC Contractors Delaware
- ABC Contractors New Jersey

MUNICIPAL GEOGRAPHIC ELEMENT

A municipal geographic element often reflects the location or origin of the company:

- Boston Market
- New York Yankees
- Philadelphia Electric Services
- Washington Post

ADVANTAGES

Here are three main advantages of a geographic name.

- First, a geographic name immediately tells your potential customers the location or scope of your business activities. This is especially true when your business name contains a municipal geographic element. This way of naming your company can attract consumers looking for a product or service in their immediate environment.
- Second, a geographic name normally facilitates the positioning of your company in search engines, including Google Local Search and Google Maps: BostonBestPlumber.com
- Finally, a geographic name can make a patriotic fiber vibrate: U.S. Best Products

DISADVANTAGES

There are also three disadvantages of a geographic name.

- First, a geographic name limits your company's ability to expand into other cities or states. Indeed, the target clientele may believe that the service or product they are looking for is only available in the city or region indicated in your company name.
- Second, a geographic name may sometimes be misunderstood by certain groups of consumers outside the region concerned.
- Finally, a geographic name is not recommended if national or international development is in your sights. Too much identification with a country or region can be problematic in case of a boycott organized in a foreign country. One must also consider the potential problems of translation quality or pronunciation ease. Finally, it is difficult to make people believe in the planetary aims of your company whose name includes the word *America* or *American*, or the initials U.S. or USA.

Finally, here are three points you should remember.

1. EXCEPTIONS

Avoid including a geographic element in your company name unless:

- You want to hit a sensitive nerve with the targeted consumer: Best Electricians Corp. of America
- Your business activities will mainly take place in a specific region of the United States: Miami Medical Center

2. CHANGE OF NAME

Some companies have changed their names, especially in order to remove the geographic connotation:

- Kentucky Fried Chicken > KFC
- Minnesota Manufacturing and Mining > 3M

3. FORTUNE 500®

About 10% of the names in the Fortune 500® directory have a geographic element.

4.3 - TEMPORAL NAME

By definition, time passes… and does not come back. Quite often, what was new yesterday is outdated today.

YEAR 2000

In the 1980s, many entrepreneurs included the number 2000 in the name of their new company. At that time, the year 2000 was still far away and represented the future:

- Construction 2000
- Sports 2000

But as soon as the new millennium was reached, it dealt a heavy blow to the old fashioned flavor.

In other words, the inclusion of a time element in your company name creates a temporary effect, which gradually deteriorates:

- In 1980, the name CREATIONS 2000 could appear avant-garde.
- In 2020, this name seems outdated.

~

But every good rule has a few exceptions.

1. YEAR OF FOUNDATION

In rare cases, it may be a good idea to include the year of foundation in your company name. For example, you want to acquire the assets of a bankrupt company, including all the rights in:

- The name of the company
- The trademark
- The domain name

To proceed with this acquisition, you want to create a new company. In such a case, it may be interesting to include the year of foundation in the name of your new company. This will allow third parties to clearly distinguish the two companies, while making them understand that the activities of the new company are related to those of the company that preceded it:

- Arica Furniture - Bankrupt company
- Arica Furniture (2020) - New company

A few years later, you will be able to change the name of your company, in order to remove the temporal particle.

2. VALUE OF THE PAST

In some cases, a reference to the past may have a positive impact.

For example, a company specializing in the sale of antique furniture will want to refer to it in its name:

- 18th Century Furniture

Finally, here are three points you should remember.

1. IN GENERAL

It is usually not recommended to include a time element in your company name.

2. DO NOT SPECIFY

If you insist on including a time element in your business name, choose a word without reference to a specific point in time:

- Century
- Eternity
- Future
- Next
- Tomorrow

3. FORTUNE 500®

Only three companies listed on the Fortune 500® directory have a time reference in their name:

- CenturyLink
- NextEra Energy
- Twenty-First Century Fox

4.4 - HISTORIC NAME

Many entrepreneurs like to look back in time to find the name of their company or part of it. Divinity and mythology are an interesting source of words and names that inspire strength, victory, power, speed, and intelligence. Gods, goddesses, and mythical creatures are very popular. Here are some names based on divinity and mythology:

Apollo: God of light, male beauty, and music

Hercules: Roman god known for his strength

Midas: Greek king known to turn everything he touched into gold

Pandora: First human woman, according to Greek mythology

Titan: Member of the second generation of divine beings

Finally, here are three points you should remember.

1. LATIN OR GREEK

If a word in everyday language is already used, why not find its equivalent in Latin or Greek? This can be very inspiring. Google Translate can help you do that.

2. MODIFICATION

It is possible to modify the name of a divinity to create a unique word. Moreover, since it is a forged word, the domain name may be easier to obtain.

- Cheops > Keops

3. FORTUNE 500®

Four companies on the Fortune 500® directory have a name that contains historical reference, intended or not.

Amazon.com

In Greek mythology, an Amazon woman was a powerful warrior. However, in this case, Jeff Bezos' inspiration probably came from the river of the same name in South America.

Nike

This is the Greek goddess of victory.

Oracle

According to Wikipedia, "... an oracle is a person or agency considered to provide wise and insightful counsel or prophetic predictions or precognition of the future, inspired by the gods".

Thor Industries

According to Wikipedia, "Thor is a hammer-wielding god associated with thunder, lightning, storms, oak trees, strength, the protection of mankind, and also hallowing and fertility."

4.5 - METAPHORIC NAME

A metaphor is a figure of speech that gives a word or expression a meaning normally attributed to another word or expression:

- *The curtain of night fell upon us.*

It is often said that a picture is worth a thousand words. Some companies have understood this perfectly:

Amazon: analogy to this great river's continuous flow

Jaguar: analogy to this feline's blazing speed

Kayak: analogy to adventure, discovery

Monster: analogy to immensity, size

~

Finally, here are three points you should remember.

1. SEVERAL METAPHORS

There are hundreds of metaphors, which can inspire you in choosing the name of your company. These are easy to find on the Internet.

2. ANALOGY

An image can sometimes have several meanings. You must therefore be well aware of the analogy you want to implant in the brains of your potential customers.

3. FORTUNE 500®

Here are some examples of metaphoric names from the Fortune 500® directory:

Arrow Electronics: direction, target, speed

Caterpillar: slowly but surely

Marathon Petroleum: long distance to cross

Oracle: infallibility

Progressive: develops step by step

Target: target to be reached - price, quality, service

4.6 - NUMERIC NAME

Everything we saw earlier in the *Numbers* section applies here. I therefore invite you to go back there, to refresh your memory.

CANADA VS. UNITED STATES

In Canada, you can get a company name consisting of numbers.

This number is automatically assigned, upon request, by the Canadian government or by one of the provincial governments:

- 124865 Canada Inc.
- 9256-7634 Québec Inc.

In the United States, this automatic assignment practice does not exist.

However, nothing prevents you from creating the numeric name of your choice, subject to its availability:

- 121936 USA Inc.
- 121936 Delaware Inc.
- 121936 Inc.

A numeric name is sometimes used by a company that will have no public activity or contact with customers:

- 141414 Holding Inc.

ADVANTAGES

There are two main advantages of a numeric name:

- First, the availability of a numeric name is almost guaranteed.
- Second, you do not have to worry about finding the name of your company.

DISADVANTAGES

There are also two main disadvantages of a numeric name:

- First, by adopting a numeric name, you will always face a potential problem of confusion or mistaken numbers, either on your part or on the part of others.
- Second, it will be impossible to ask your customers to memorize a numeric name.

Finally, here are three points you should remember.

1. FEELING

A numeric name does not give your potential customers any particular feelings in their minds.

2. EVERYTHING BUT...

Any business name will be a lot better than a numeric name.

3. FORTUNE 500®

No company listed in the Fortune 500® directory has a numeric name. That means everything.

4.7 - NAME IN FOREIGN LANGUAGE

It may be interesting if your company name consists of one or more words from a foreign language:

- Cirque du Soleil
- Häagen-Dazs
- Volkswagen
- Volvo

MEANING

When you create an American company, government authorities will generally ask you for the meaning of the word or words in a language other than English—unless they are the same or similar in both languages.

Indeed, the state that will create your company wants to avoid any troubled situation that may result from the meaning of the words in question. For example, if an English word is prohibited in your company's name, so will be its foreign language equivalent.

. . .

Also, if you make a mistake in the name written in a foreign language, do not rely on government authorities to correct your mistake. That is not their role. Instead, you will need to file a request to amend your company's certificate of creation.

IDENTICAL WORDS EN-FR

Some words are spelled in the same way in English (EN) and French (FR).

Most of these words are true friends, because their meaning is identical or almost the same in both languages. Even if the spelling is the same, the pronunciation is often somewhat different.

- Orange
- Robot
- Table
- Television
- Zoo

But some words are false friends, because they do not have the same meaning in the other language.

- Change > EN: transform | FR: currency
- Coin > EN: currency | FR: corner
- Confidence > EN: trust | FR: secret
- Habit > EN: routine | FR: clothing
- Queue > EN: waiting line | FR: tail

SIMILAR WORDS EN-FR

Other words are spelled in almost the same way in both languages. Often, only a few characters distinguish them.

- Address - Adresse
- Apartment - Appartement
- Comfort - Confort
- Envelope - Enveloppe

SIMILAR WORDS EN-EN

Sometimes, some words are spelled in almost the same way, in the same language, but in two different countries.

- USA: Check | Canada: Cheque
- USA: Color | Canada: Colour
- USA: Dialog | Canada: Dialogue
- USA: Favorite | Canada: Favourite
- USA: Labor | Canada: Labour

ADVANTAGES

The advantage of a name in a foreign language is simple. The sight and sound of such a name will generally attract attention:

- Cirque du Soleil
- Hyundai

DISADVANTAGES

However, the major disadvantage of a company name in a foreign language is its meaning. Such a name can have a negative or pejorative meaning in some languages.

For example, the name of some products sold by Ikea in the past had a sexual connotation in the Thai language.

For its part, when the Chevrolet manufacturer launched the Chevy Nova car, it probably did not know that Nova means *it doesn't go* in Spanish.

Finally, the manufacturer Mitsubishi had to rename its vehicle Pajero in Spanish-speaking countries, because for them, this word means *who masturbates often.*

Another disadvantage is that pronouncing a word in a foreign language can sometimes be difficult for an English-speaking person.

Finally, here are three points you should remember.

1. SEVERAL LANGUAGES

If you wish to use a word in a language other than English, you must know the meaning of this word in several languages. Google Translate can help you do that.

2. KNOWN WORDS

Some French words are well known and used in the United States:

- Boutique
- Chauffeur
- Chic
- Croissant
- Entrepreneur
- Fiancé
- Souvenir

3. FORTUNE 500®

At least 49 company names in the Fortune 500® directory have an identical word in French.

4.8 - DOMAIN NAME

To learn more about your company, one of your potential customers' first instincts will be to research it on the Internet.

If the domain name is part of your company name, you will immediately provide these potential customers with its virtual address.

PRODUCTS AND SERVICES

A domain name is often used for companies, but also for their products and services. Here are some examples:

Amazon

- Main domain name: amazon.com
- Related domain names: alexa.com, kindle.com, prime.com

Apple

- Main domain name: apple.com
- Related domain names: iphone.com, ipod.com, macbookpro.com

Microsoft

- Main domain name: microsoft.com
- Related domain names: bing.com, office.com, windows.com

SLOGANS

A domain name sometimes refers to a company's slogan.

For example, the firm EY — formerly Ernst & Young — uses the slogan *Building a better working world.* It has therefore reserved several dozen similar domain names, including the following:

- buildingabetterworkingworld.com
- betterworkingworld.com

All these domain names are redirected to the main domain name *ey.com*.

Finally, here are three points you should remember.

1. BRILLIANT!

Few entrepreneurs dare to include a domain name in their company name. Yet this strategy is brilliant, because it provides two pieces of information at once: the name of the company and its virtual address.

- Amazon.com
- Lynda.com
- Salesforce.com

2. BUSINESS NAME

If you decide to use a domain name as your business name:

- First, make sure the domain name ends with the .com extension. Otherwise, your potential customers will often make the mistake of indicating .com instead of the extension you have chosen. This will create constant confusion with a website other than yours. However, this statement must be qualified if the extension used is strong in your country - for example, .ca in Canada, .fr in France, etc..
- Second, always provide the full name of your company. For example, if you choose *Gogopro.com* as your company name, always mention *Gogopro.com* and not its shortened version *Gogopro*.
- Finally, never forget to renew your domain name before it expires. Otherwise, you will likely be forced to change your company name. Even worse, you will lose the traffic associated with your old domain name.

3. FORTUNE 500®

Only two companies listed in the Fortune 500® directory use the strategy of including a domain name in their company name:

- Amazon.com
- salesforce.com

4.9 - ASSUMED NAME

As we have seen previously, an assumed name is a trade name under which a company does business and is different from its legal name.

For example, ABC Inc. uses the assumed name Gogopro. So we will say:

- ABC Inc. *doing business as* Gogopro
- ABC Inc. *dba* Gogopro

In the United States, the assumed name is known in various ways:

- Alias Name
- Assumed Name
- Business Name
- DBA Name
- Fictitious Name
- Trade Name

WHY AN ASSUMED NAME?

Here are some examples regarding the use of an assumed name.

1. An individual wishes to carry on a business under a name other than his or her own, without having to create a separate legal entity — such as a corporation or an LLC. For example, *Bob's Garage* or *Nancy's Restaurant.*

2. A company wants to operate a website under a name other than its own. For example, ABC Inc. operates a website under the name *Gogopro*. Its online shop sells everyday consumer products. The consumers can place an order and pay with their credit card. On their monthly card statement, the consumers expect to see the name *Gogopro*, since it is the name of the online store. If the consumers see *ABC Inc.* instead, they will not necessarily make the link between this company and the *Gogopro* store. By attaching the *Gogopro* alias to its own name, ABC Inc. may therefore see *Gogopro* appear on its customers' card statements.

3. A company wants to operate several websites, each with a different name.

4. A company wants to operate several divisions, without having to create a new legal entity for each of them.

PROCESS FOR OBTAINING AN ASSUMED NAME

The process for obtaining an assumed name in the United States varies from state to state. For example:

- In the state of Delaware, the application for an assumed name is made at the county level. There are three counties in this state.
- In Florida, the application for an assumed name is made at the state level.

The cost for obtaining an assumed name generally varies between $10 and $100.

In some cases, a state or county may require you to publish a notice in newspapers, to notify third parties of the existence of the assumed name. Then, you will have to file an affidavit with the state confirming the publication.

The time required to register an assumed name varies from a few minutes to 30 days, depending on the state or county.

DURATION OF AN ASSUMED NAME

The duration of registration of the assumed name also varies by state and county:

- In some cases, the assumed name remains in force as long as an application to cancel the registration is not filed.
- In other cases, the registration of an assumed name is valid for a specific period of time — for example, five years. A renewal application must therefore be filed before the registration expires.

Finally, here are three points you should remember.

1. LOW PROTECTION

American lawyers consider that the legal protection granted to an assumed name is particularly weak. They therefore suggest that this protection be increased by filing a trademark with the United States Patent and Trademark Office - USPTO.

2. LEGAL IDENTIFIER

An assumed name generally cannot contain the legal identifiers reserved for companies — for example, Inc., Corp., Ltd., LLC, etc.

3. BANK ACCOUNT

Some U.S. banks do not want to associate more than one assumed name per bank account. In such a case, if your company wants to use several assumed names, you will probably need to open more than one bank account.

4.10 - DESCRIPTIVE NAME

A descriptive name is a name that contains at least one common dictionary word, and describes the nature of a company's activities.

- Bob Flooring
- ABC Hamburgers & Fries

ADVANTAGES

There are two main advantages of a descriptive name:

- First, a descriptive name simplifies the effort required to associate your company name with the nature of its activities.
- Second, the keywords contained in your company name can potentially become useful in search engines.

DISADVANTAGES

However, the disadvantages associated with a descriptive name are more numerous:

- First, a descriptive name has no distinctive character. Nothing can prevent your competitors from using the same keywords in their names or advertisements. For example, the words *Best Buy* are often used in advertising in the United States, despite a chain of stores with the same name.
- Second, a descriptive name will not evoke any particular emotion in the minds of your potential customers.
- Third, a descriptive name is limiting, whereas your company can generally carry out several different activities. For example, *ABC Landscaping* is a limiting name if the company then wants to also offer snow removal services.
- Fourth, a descriptive name invariably involves significant costs, in the event of a subsequent change in your company name.

Finally, here are three points you should remember.

1. TEMPTATION

Resist the temptation to choose a name that describes the nature of the services or products your company intends to offer. One day, you will regret it. In addition, how will you distinguish your company from your competitors', if its name is only descriptive?

- McDonald's Corp. vs. Hamburgers & Fries Inc.

2. DISTINCTIVE WORD

If you still insist on including one or more descriptive words in your company name, make sure that it contains at least one distinctive word.

3. FORTUNE 500®

Nearly 6% of U.S. companies listed in the Fortune 500® directory do not have a particularly distinctive name. These names contain common dictionary words, which describe in whole or in part the nature of the company's activities. However, it should be noted that these are companies that have existed for a long time, when the way of naming a company was not yet a widespread science.

Here is the list of these company names:

- Air Products & Chemicals
- American Axle & Manufacturing
- American Electric Power
- American Family Insurance Group
- American Financial Group
- Applied Materials
- Auto-Owners Insurance
- Dollar General
- Enterprise Products Partners
- General Electric
- General Mills
- General Motors
- Genuine Parts
- Global Partners
- Intercontinental Exchange
- International Paper
- Laboratory Corp. of America
- News Corp.
- Occidental Petroleum
- Packaging Corp. of America
- Public Service Enterprise Group
- Tractor Supply
- United Natural Foods
- United Rentals

- United States Steel
- Universal Health Services
- US Foods Holding
- Waste Management
- World Fuel Services

4.11 - DISTINCTIVE NAME

A distinctive business name is a name that clearly distinguishes your company from its competitors. There are at least five methods for obtaining a distinctive name.

The **first method** is to forge a name from existing words:

- CorpoMax > Corporation + Maximum
- Equifax > Equitable + Factual
- Evernote > Forever + Note
- Groupon > Group + Coupon
- Microsoft > Microcomputer + Software
- Qualcomm > Quality + Communications

The **second method** is to modify an existing word:

* By replacing a letter

- Googol > Google
- Rumba > Roomba

* By adding a letter

- Phone > iPhone
- Pad > iPad
- Robot > iRobot

* By removing a letter

- Flicker > Flickr
- Tumbler > Tumblr

* By repeating a letter

- Fiver > Fiverr
- Muffins > Mmmuffins

The **third method** is to create a word without any particular meaning:

- Kleenex
- Kodak
- Skype
- Xerox

The **fourth method** is to choose a word that has no relation to the products or services offered by the company:

- Amazon
- Apple

The **last method** is to attach two words in an original or interesting way:

- Facebook
- PayPal
- YouTube

ADVANTAGES

There are many advantages of a distinctive company name.

First, according to several American lawyers, the legal protection granted to a distinctive name is generally greater than that granted to a name composed of common words in the dictionary.

Second, the risk of confusion between a distinctive name and another name is lower, especially in the minds of your potential customers.

Third, a distinctive business name makes it much easier to obtain various other names:

- Domain name
- Trademark
- Username on social networks

Fourth, a distinctive name evokes emotion and facilitates memorization.

Finally, a distinctive name offers you flexibility when it comes to adding, removing, or modifying your company's activities. What your company does today does not necessarily represent what it will do tomorrow.

DISADVANTAGES

As for the disadvantages of a distinctive company name, there may only be one: it can sometimes cost you more to make your company name known.

Finally, here are three points you should remember.

1. UNDER THE NAME

Indicate the nature of your company's activities under its name, not in its name. Do it everywhere: website, business cards, documentation, etc. In the future, if the nature of your company's activities changes or expands, you will not need to change its name. Only the description attached to your company name will be modified, usually at a low cost.

2. WEB TOOLS

In the *Useful Resources* section, you will find several web-based tools to help you find your company name.

3. FORTUNE 500®

Several companies listed in the Fortune 500® directory have a distinctive name, including:

- Apple
- Coca-Cola
- Comcast
- Costco
- Exxon Mobil
- FedEx
- Microsoft
- Netflix
- Nike
- Qualcomm
- Verizon
- Virgin
- Walmart
- Xerox

Their names usually do not contain any descriptive part. Thus, customers' attention is focused exclusively on the distinctive aspect of the name. On the other hand, their name is often used in conjunction with a slogan. It is obvious that their financial resources allow these companies to devote a large part of their budget to advertising and marketing.

4.12 - MILITARY NAME

The United States is a country with one of the most powerful military forces in the world. Americans have a deep respect for those who protect and defend them in armed conflicts.

The U.S. armed military structure has six branches:

- Air Force
- Army
- Coast Guard
- Marine Corps
- Navy
- Space Force

Some companies have understood this national attachment to the uniform. They therefore use words from the military dictionary.

NAMES WITH A MILITARY CONNOTATION

Here are some examples of names with a military connotation:

- Air Force > Air Force Achievements
- Army > Salvation Army
- Arrow > Arrow Design House
- Brigade > Brigade Engineering
- Bullet > Bullet Marketing
- Captain > Captain Crunch
- Commander > Commander Drilling
- General > General Commander
- Marine > Marine Supply
- Navy > Navy Adventures
- Rocket > Rocket Mortgage
- Sabre > Buffalo Sabres
- Squad > Squad Productions
- Target > Target Stores
- Victory > Victory Brewing
- Weapon > Weapons of Mass Production

IDEAS CONVEYED

Here are some ideas conveyed by certain words with a military connotation, including *Brigade*, *Squad,* and *Army*:

- Confidence
- Discipline
- Effort
- Organization
- Teamwork
- Thoroughness

CONTROLLED USE

Some U.S. states may control the use of company names that include the words *Marines* - plural -, *Air Force,* and *Coast Guard*. The control seems less pronounced for the words *Army* and *Navy*, because they are part of the common language.

Finally, here are three points you should remember.

1. REAL ESTATE

Military words are often popular among companies that provide services to building owners:

- Cleaning > Maid Brigade
- Lawn care > Lawn Army
- Moving services > Two Marines Moving
- Snow removal > Snow Squad
- Window cleaning > Squeegee Squad

2. TRADEMARKS

Do not forget to check the U.S. trademark directory on the United States Patent and Trademark Office website — uspto.gov — before choosing a name with a military connotation. You will discover that the American military divisions own several trademarks:

- U.S. Marine Corps and Navy: nearly 700
- Army: nearly 300
- Air Force: over 70
- Coast Guard: over 15

3. FORTUNE 500®

In the Fortune 500® directory, the names of two companies contain a word that may suggest it is part of the military dictionary:

- Arrow Electronics
- Target

In addition, six company names include the word *General*. However, it is rather in the common sense than military that this word must be interpreted:

- Casey's General Stores
- Dollar General
- General Dynamics
- General Electric
- General Mills
- General Motors

In short, words with a military connotation are not popular among large American companies.

4.13 - RELIGIOUS OR CHARITABLE NAME

In the United States, religion has always been omnipresent. It is therefore not surprising that some American companies have adopted a name with a religious or charitable reference. Here are some words used in this sense:

- Angel
- Bible
- Bishop
- Chaplain
- Church
- Compassion
- Cross
- Crusader
- Deacon
- Demon
- Devil
- Divinity
- Faith
- Friar
- Goodwill

- Holly
- Hope
- Knight
- Lord
- Memorial
- Mercy
- Monarch
- Mission
- Pastor
- Preachers
- Priest
- Redemption
- Relief
- Saint | St.
- Salvation
- Samaritan

NON-PROFIT ORGANIZATIONS

A name with a religious or charitable connotation is often used by non-profit organizations:

Churches

- Church of the Resurrection
- Redemption Church
- St. Martin's Episcopal Church

Hospitals

- Bon Secours St. Francis Hospital
- Good Samaritan Hospital
- Mercy Hospital
- Saint Alphonsus Medical Center
- St. Jude Children's Research Hospital

Educational Institutions

- St. Mary's Seminary and University
- University of Notre Dame

Charitable Organizations

- Catholic Charities USA
- Goodwill
- Samaritan's Purse
- The Salvation Army

SPORT TEAMS

A name with a religious or charitable connotation is also used by some for-profit companies, such as sports teams:

Baseball

- Los Angeles Angels
- San Diego Padres

Football

- New Orleans Saints

Hockey

- Las Vegas Golden Knights
- New Jersey Devils

ADVANTAGES

The only real advantage of a business name with a religious or charitable connotation is to make a sensitive fiber vibrate in some consumers.

DISADVANTAGES

However, there are two main disadvantages.

First, such a company name may alienate other consumers, whose religious beliefs differ from yours.

Second, the use of the word *Saint* in a company name is often problematic. How are you going to write it: Saint? St? With a hyphen? Without a hyphen? With a period? Without a period?

- Saint Jude
- Saint-Jude
- St Jude
- St-Jude
- St. Jude
- St.Jude

In both long and short versions, the use of the word *Saint* in a company name leads to inconsistency in the minds of the clientele. How will your customers write it or even remember how to write it?

Do you want to spend the rest of your professional life spelling out your company name? To indicate whether or not there is a hyphen, a dot, or a space?

Finally, here are three points you should remember.

1. THINK ABOUT IT

Think carefully before choosing a name with a religious or charitable reference. This may make sense if you are starting a church. Not necessarily if you sell hunting and fishing gear.

2. DOMAIN NAME

If you still choose a name with the long or short version of the word *Saint*, it is preferable to reserve several variations of the domain name.

For example, if you choose the company name *St. Vincent Flowers*, it will be wise to reserve domain names with variations of the word *Saint*:

- StVincentFlowers.com
- St-VincentFlowers.com
- StVincent-Flowers.com
- St-Vincent-Flowers.com
- SaintVincentFlowers.com
- Saint-VincentFlowers.com
- SaintVincent-Flowers.com
- Saint-Vincent-Flowers.com

Then you can choose the main domain name and redirect others to it.

For its part, the St. Jude Children's Research Hospital failed to — or could not — adequately protect its domain name.

Domain name belonging to the hospital

- stjude.org

Domain names belonging to others

- st-jude.org
- stjude.com

- st-jude.com

- stjude.net
- st-jude.net

3. FORTUNE 500®

No company name in the Fortune 500® directory includes the word *Saint* or the abbreviation *St.* However, two company names have a religious or divine reference, intended or not:

- Cardinal Health
- Oracle

4.14 - SUPERLATIVE NAME

Many people like to use superlatives in their communications:

- The best chocolate
- The most beautiful car
- The king of hamburgers

In business, it can be interesting to position your company high in the minds of its current and potential customers.

POWER WORDS

Using certain words in your company name can help you get that ultimate position. These words bring to mind power or the summit and are referred to as power words.

Here are some examples:

A+

- A+ House Cleaning
- A+ Printing

A-1

- A-1 Cleaner
- A-1 Garage

Apex

- Apex Aeronautics
- Apex Cinema

Best

- Best Auto Deals
- Best Buy
- Best Liquors

Better

- Better Title Loans
- Better Maid House Cleaning

Big

- Big 8 Supermarket
- Big K
- Big Mac

Cap

- Cap Consulting
- Cap Development

Chef

- Chef Boy-Ar-Dee

- The Spicy Chef

Crest

- Crest Construction
- Crest Logistics

Crown

- Crown Motel
- Crown Pizza

Expert

- Bartlett Tree Experts
- HR Business Expert

Extra

- Extra Grocery
- Extra Space Storage

First — 1st

- First Delaware Financial
- FirstEnergy
- 1st Class Glass
- 1st IT Solutions

Grand

- Grand Food Services
- Grand General Contractor

Hyper

- Hyper Active
- Hyper Bicycles

King

- Burger King
- King Garden Restaurant

Leader

- Leader Paper Products
- Leaders Insurance Group
- Our Future Leaders Academy

Master

- Mastercard
- Master Tile and Carpets
- Master Shower Doors

Max

- CarMax
- CorpoMax

Mega

- Mega Dollar
- Mega Wireless

Most

- Most Holy Family Monastery

- Most Influential Magazine

One — 1

- Auto One
- Capital One
- Cleaner One
- Group 1 Automotive

Peak

- Peak Acquisition
- Peak Adventure

Pinnacle

- Pinnacle Biologics
- Pinnacle Flowers

Plus +

- Auto Plus
- Car Wash +
- Pet Supplies Plus

Preferred

- Preferred Home Inspections
- Preferred Tax Services

Premium

- Piazza Premium Automobiles
- Premium Healthcare

Queen

- Dairy Queen
- Queen Media

Royal

- Royal Farms
- Royal Prestige

Sky

- Sky Coffee
- Sky High Adventures

Summit

- Summit Aviation
- Summit Condominiums

Super

- Parivar Supermarket
- Super Spirits
- Supervalu

Supra

- Supra Computers
- Supra Lawn & Landscaping

Tip

- Tip Mobile
- Tip Productions

Tip Top

- Tip Top Entertainment
- Tip Top Foods

Top

- Top Hats
- Top Nails

Total

- Total Fitness
- Total Wine
- Total Wireless

Ultra

- Ultra Car Center
- Ultra Nail Studio

Vertex

- Vertex Finance
- Vertex Fitness

Zenith

- Zenith Auto Parts
- Zenith Communications

QUANTITY

Superlative words that evoke quantity can also be used.

Here are some examples:

& Beyond

- Banana Shoes & Beyond
- Bed, Bath & Beyond

& More

- Carpet & More
- Flowers & More
- Parcels & More
- Tools & More
- Total Wine & More

& Things

- Birthday Cakes & Things
- Philly Wings & Things
- Toys & Things

Above & Beyond

- Above & Beyond Cruises Vacations
- Above & Beyond Unisex Hair Salon

ADVANTAGES

There are two main advantages of a superlative name:

- First, a superlative name can create a positive impression in the minds of potential customers.
- Second, the use of such a name can also increase the scope of one or more descriptive words.

DISADVANTAGES

Now, here are some disadvantages:

- First, superlative words are overused. This sometimes makes them less credible in the minds of consumers.
- Second, superlative words are not distinctive in themselves, as they are composed of common words.
- Finally, as we saw in the *Special Characters* section, using an ampersand— for example, *& Beyond*—is problematic in a domain name. It must be replaced by the word *and*, which distorts the name of the company.

Finally, here are three points you should remember.

1. MARKETING

Generally, a large marketing budget must support a superlative name:

- Bed Bath & Beyond
- Best Buy

2. CONFUSION

It is easy for a superlative name to be confused:

- Best Wings & Things
- Philly Wings & Things
- Wings & Things

3. FORTUNE 500®

Only eleven Fortune 500® companies have a name with a superlative word:

- Bed Bath & Beyond
- Best Buy
- Builders FirstSource
- Crown Holdings
- First American Financial
- First Data
- FirstEnergy
- Group 1 Automotive
- Mastercard
- Publix Super Markets
- Supervalu

4.15 - NAME WITH INITIALS

As we saw in the *Initialisms and Acronyms* section, the use of initials in a company name is generally not recommended. However, this way of naming a company is still widely used in the United States. As previously discussed, several mature companies have decided to shorten their name. The preferred method was generally to use the initials of the words in their original name. Again, here are some examples:

- America Online > AOL
- Dairy Queen > DQ
- Hewlett Packard > HP
- International Business Machines > IBM
- Kentucky Fried Chicken > KFC
- Minnesota Mining and Manufacturing Co. > 3M
- United Parcel Service > UPS
- Weight Watchers > WW

Finally, here are three points you should remember.

1. PERIODS OR SPACES

If you absolutely want to insert initials in your company name, do not put any period or space between the letters. In any case, your customers and suppliers will not.

2. BING

Before launching its own search engine, Microsoft invested millions of dollars to ensure that the name *BING* would be acceptable anywhere in the world, in all languages. However, Microsoft probably did not foresee the transformation by some of the word *BING* into an acronym for *But It's Not Google.*

3. FORTUNE 500®

Nearly 14% of the names in the Fortune 500® directory - 67 companies - have initials.

Ten company names have the initials of a first name—which is an old way of naming a company:

- Arthur J. Gallagher
- C.H. Robinson Worldwide
- D.R. Horton
- J.B. Hunt Transport Services
- J.C. Penney
- J.M. Smucker
- JPMorgan Chase
- R.R. Donnelley & Sons
- W.R. Berkley
- W.W. Grainger

Five company names have initials separated by an ampersand:

- AT&T
- BB&T
- M&T Bank Corp.
- PG&E Corp.
- S&P Global

4.16 - NAME WITH GREETING

In general, politeness is essential. It attracts the eye, charms the ear, and forges relationships. Several companies have understood the importance of their positioning in this regard in the minds of their potential customers.

ELEMENTS OF GREETING

Greetings often find their place in the names or brands of companies. Here are some examples:

Mr.

- Mr. Clean
- Mr. Freeze
- Mr. Handyman
- Mr. John
- Mr. Muffler
- Mr. Tire
- Mr. Transmission

Mister

- Mister Discount Homes
- Mister Music

Miss

- Miss Heather's School of Dance
- Miss Karen's Home Day Care
- Miss Oxford Diner

Mrs.

- Mrs. Juice
- Mrs. Tickets

Sir

- Sir Lancelot Courier
- Sir Speedy

DOCTOR

However, the element of greeting that beats all others is undoubtedly the title of doctor. Here are some examples:

Dr.

- Dr. Auto Repair
- Dr. Pepper
- Dr. Scholl
- Dr. Vinyl

Doctor

- Auto Doctor
- Glass Doctor
- Lawn Doctor

Doc

- Doc Smithers B&B
- Doc Watson's Home Inspection

ADVANTAGES

The main advantage of a name with a salutation element is to positively position your company in the minds of its potential customers.

DISADVANTAGES

However, there are at least two important disadvantages:

- First, your potential customers will not know how to write or search the Internet for what they hear. Short version or long version of Mister? Short version or long version of Doctor?
- Second, this way of naming a company is frequently used, which dilutes its interest.

Finally, here are three points you should remember.

1. INTERESTING

In some circumstances, adding a greeting element to your company name may be interesting. It all depends on the industry in which your company will operate and its competitive environment.

2. MASCULINE VS. FEMININE

The use of a masculine greeting element — Mr. — or a professional salutation — Dr. — is very popular in the repair and maintenance services industries.

The use of a feminine greeting element - Mrs., Ms., Miss - is not as popular, except in the area of education and child care services.

3. FORTUNE 500®

In the Fortune 500® directory, Dr Pepper Snapple Group is the only company that uses a greeting element in its name.

4.17 - HUMOROUS NAME

In general, people like humor. It is more pleasant to laugh than to cry.

In business, some entrepreneurs have chosen to name their company with humor. In certain circumstances, this choice can be interesting:

Cleaning

- Spruce Springclean

Fans

- Big Ass Fans

Hairdressing salon

- I'll Cut You Hair Studio

Mexican restaurant

- Tequila Mockingbird

Musical instrument store

- Crazy Dave's Music

Seafood restaurant

- Frying Nemo Fish & Chip Restaurant

Thai restaurant

- Thai Tanic

But if you want to be taken seriously, or if you are in a serious field, it is better that your company name be taken seriously as well. For example, companies offering professional services — lawyers, accountants, engineers, architects, etc. — cannot risk using a humorous name. Moreover, the professional associations of which they are members normally govern the use of their business name.

Finally, here are three points you should remember.

1. WEB TOOLS

In the *Useful Resources* section, you will find some web-based tools to find a funny or humorous company name.

2. ERA

A name can be funny at a certain time, less funny a little later. For example, take the case of the *Frying Nemo* restaurant. In 30 years' time, will this humorous reference resonate so much in the minds of consumers who have not seen this - old - movie?

3. FORTUNE 500®

No company listed in the Fortune 500® directory has a funny or humorous name. However, some names are original, but nothing more:

- Bed Bath & Beyond
- Toys "R" Us

4.18 - ACTION NAME

Some company and brand names contain words that imply action. These words are often:

Verbs used in imperative mode

- 1-800-Go-FedEx
- Go Daddy
- GoPro
- PayPal

Verbs used in indicative mode

- Blinds To Go
- Wings To Go

Names synonymous with action or adventure

- Explorer
- Safari

ADVANTAGES

A company name with an action word has at least two advantages:

- First, it includes a clear and direct call for your customers to take action.
- Second, it stimulates the brain and memory of people who see or hear it.

DISADVANTAGES

However, you must consider two important disadvantages:

- First, an action name consists of common words from the dictionary.
- Second, an action name can only become truly distinctive over time and with a large advertising budget.

Finally, here are three points you should remember.

1. POPULAR

Business names involving an action are generally popular and stand the test of time quite well.

2. BRANDS

Curiously, words involving action are more often used in brands than company names.

3. FORTUNE 500®

Only seven companies in the Fortune 500® directory have a name that implies a call or reference to the action:

- American Express
- Discover Financial Services
- Discovery
- Expedia Group
- PayPal Holdings
- Travelers
- Visa

This is normal because action-based company names have become popular only in recent years.

4.19 - POSITIVE NAME

People have always been attracted to the positive. Words that have a positive connotation are often those related to the following elements:

Assistance

- Rite Aid

Authenticity

- Genuine Parts

Dynamism

- Steel Dynamics

Family

- American Family Insurance Group
- Simon & Sons
- Smith Brothers

Friendship

- Friendly's

Happiness

- Happier at Home Pet Care
- Happiness Gift Baskets

Health

- Healthy Smiles of Delaware
- Mona's Health Foods

Humanity

- Humana

Innovation

- Advancing Strategic Innovations
- Pioneer Natural Resources

Intelligence

- BrightHouse

Joy

- Hands of Joy Beauty Salon
- Joy Through Yoga

Liberty

- Liberty Mutual Insurance Group

Loyalty

- Fidelity National Financial

Neighborhood

- Good Neighbors Home Repair

Performance

- Performance Food Group

Prudence

- Prudential Financial
- Progressive

Public service

- Public Service Enterprise Group

Quality

- Best Buy
- Quality is Our Recipe

Resources

- Targa Resources

Security

- Securian Financial Group
- Securitas

Smiles

- Smiley's

Solutions

- Motorola Solutions

Success

- Success Driving School
- Successful Project Consulting

Teamwork

- Auto Team Delaware
- Enterprise Products Partners
- Goldman Sachs Group

Trust

- Reliance Steel & Aluminum
- SunTrust Banks

Unity

- United Technologies
- Walgreens Boots Alliance

Value

- Supervalu

Well-being

- Mc Kean Wellness Center
- WellCare Health Plans

Some company names have more than one positive word:

- Liberty Mutual Insurance Group
- Performance Food Group

ADVANTAGES

Do not underestimate the main advantage of a positive word in your company name: to strike a sensitive nerve among your potential customers.

DISADVANTAGES

However, a major disadvantage is that some positive words are overused:

- Group
- Partners

~

Finally, here are three points you should remember.

1. MODIFY

You can change a positive name to make it distinctive, while still maintaining its appeal to your target audience:

- Humana
- Securian

- Securitas

2. NEGATIVE NAMES

Some names that are considered negative can nevertheless attract attention:

- Poison - perfume brand
- The Boring Company - an Elon Musk company

3. FORTUNE 500®

More than 40 businesses in the Fortune 500® directory have a name with a positive connotation. Here are some of them:

- Best Buy
- Cognizant Technology Solutions
- Fidelity National Financial
- Genuine Parts
- Liberty Media
- Rite Aid
- WellCare Health Plans

4.20 - ANIMAL NAME

Many company and brand names contain the name of an animal. Often, the animal has been selected for one or more of its characteristics, personality traits, or character traits.

Here are some examples of animal names - real or modified - by field of activity:

Agricultural Equipment

- John Deere
- Caterpillar

Alcoholic Beverages

- Grey Goose

Automobile

- Aries
- Barracuda
- Beetle

- Bluebird
- Bobcat
- Bronco
- Cobra
- Cougar
- Eagle
- Falcon
- Fox
- Hornet
- Impala
- Jaguar
- Lynx
- Marlin
- Mangusta
- Mustang
- Pantera
- Pinto
- Puma
- Rabbit
- Ram
- Roadrunner
- Stingray
- Taurus
- Viper
- Wildcat

Beauty Care Products

- Dove

Energy Drinks

- RedBull

Grocery Stores

- Wawa

Insurance

- Geico

Passenger Transport

- Greyhound

Refurbished Electronic Products

- Gazelle

Sports Clothing and Shoes

- Puma
- Reebok

Telephone Services

- Fido
- Grasshopper

Web Browsers

- Firefox

Web Services

- MailChimp
- PicMonkey

MASCOT

Sometimes, a company does not necessarily use an animal name in its own name, but adopts an animal as its official mascot. The animal becomes in a way the image of the company. It invariably attracts attention, which is the ultimate goal of any advertising campaign. Here are some examples:

Alligator

- HostGator

Bird

- Twitter

Bull

- Red Bull

Butterfly

- MSN

Cat

- Eveready
- Friskies

Cheetah

- Cheetos

Cow

- The Laughing Cow

Crocodile

- Lacoste

Dog

- Bush's Baked Beans
- Slush Puppie

Duck

- Aflac

Gecko

- Geico

Horse

- Budweiser

Monkey

- MailChimp

Mouse

- Disney

Owl

- Hootsuite
- TripAdvisor

Panda

- World Wide Fund for Nature

Penguin

- Linux

Polar Bear

- Coca-Cola

Rabbit or Hare

- Duracell
- Energizer
- Nesquik

Rooster

- Kellogg's Corn Flakes

Tiger

- Kellogg's Frosted Flakes

ADVANTAGES

There are three main advantages to using an animal name:

- First, it creates a nice, endearing image in the minds of your customers.
- Second, it allows you to create interesting and catchy logos. A picture is worth a thousand words.
- Finally, it does not confine your company to a particular area of activity.

DISADVANTAGES

On the downside, some may find it childish or inappropriate to associate the name or image of an animal with a commercial enterprise.

Finally, here are three points you should remember.

1. IDEAS FOR NAMES

In the *Useful Resources* section, you will find a list of name idea generators, some of which are related to animal names.

2. SUGGESTIONS

Some websites suggest company and domain names related to animals.

3. FORTUNE 500®

Only four companies in the Fortune 500® directory have a name that includes an animal name — voluntarily or not:

- Caterpillar
- Cisco Systems
- Deere
- Devon

5 - HOW TO CHOOSE YOUR BUSINESS NAME

5.1 - THE 8 ESSENTIAL TOOLS

To build a house, you need tools. To find the name of your company, you also need tools. Some of them will be used more than others, but you should be familiar with all of them.

1. SEARCH ENGINES

The first tool is undoubtedly all search engines. When you start the process leading to the choice of the company name, your first instinct will probably be to browse the web. There are currently four main search engines:

Google

The most important search engine is Google. This web giant offers various levels of research, including the following:

- Simple search
- Advanced search
- Search by image

Bing

The second search engine is Bing. Owned by Microsoft, it offers similar functions to those of Google. Bing feeds in particular AOL and Yahoo! search engines.

Amazon

The third search engine is Amazon. Unknown as such, but probably one of the most powerful, Amazon's website is an excellent way to find out if the company or brand name you have chosen is already in use. In addition to the U.S. site amazon.com, you should also visit its affiliated sites, including amazon.fr, amazon.ca, etc.

YouTube

Finally, the fourth search engine is YouTube. Owned by Google, this video distribution channel is another search giant.

2. DICTIONARIES

The second tool is the set of dictionaries. To find your company name, the dictionary is undoubtedly one of the most important tools. Most online dictionaries provide one or more of the following services:

- Definitions
- Examples
- Synonyms
- Translations

In the *Useful Resources* section, you will find a list of dictionaries that will help you.

3. NAME CREATION SITES

The third tool is the set of websites that help you create names. There are dozens of websites offering you the possibility to create or find a company or brand name. Of course, these tools are not perfect, but they can provide you with the inspiration you need. In the *Useful Resources* section, you will find several sites to help you create names.

4. SOCIAL NETWORKS

The fourth tool is the set of social networks. These are a source of information that should not be underestimated. By consulting these social networks, you can check whether the username you prefer - ideally similar to the company's name - is available. In the *Useful Resources* section, you will find a list of the most popular social networks in the United States.

5. BUSINESS REGISTERS

The fifth tool is the set of business registers in the United States. To find out if the name chosen for your company is available, it is important to consult the register of the state in which it will be created. In the United States, there are 50 states as well as the District of Columbia. It is often advantageous to entrust this name availability search to a specialized firm. Indeed, some states analyze the risk of confusion between the proposed name and existing names. Other states do not do so and accept any name that is not identical to existing names.

6. TRADEMARK REGISTERS

The sixth tool is the set of trademark registers. The name you want for your company may be available on a state registry. But what if the chosen name has already been registered as a trademark, in relation to products or services similar to those your company will offer? Therefore, it may be wise - not to say careful - to consult the trademark register in the countries where you are considering doing business. In the *Useful Resources* section, you will find a list of the main trademark registries in the United States and abroad.

7. DOMAIN NAME REGISTERS

The seventh tool is the set of domain name registries. When you choose the name of your company, it is crucial to ensure that the corresponding domain name is also available. In the *Useful Resources* section, you will find a list of the major domain name registrars in the United States. Their websites include a quick search tool, usually called WHOIS.

8. YOURSELF

The eighth tool is by far the most important. It is yourself, that is to say:

- Your brain
- Your emotions
- Your experience
- Your heart
- Your instinct
- Your intelligence
- Your intuition
- Your knowledge
- Your perception
- Your subconscious

Never underestimate yourself!

Finally, here are three points you should remember.

1. GOOGLE TRANSLATE AND DEEPL

For years, my favorite tool has been *Google Translate*.

- First, it offers a translation service in more than 85 languages.
- Second, it allows you to listen to the pronunciation of a word, expression, or sentence in most of these languages.
- Third, it often provides several definitions of the same word.
- Finally, it provides a series of synonyms.

However, I recently discovered DeepL. Launched in August 2017, this online tool uses artificial intelligence to deliver high-quality translations.

2. USE

It is good to have tools, but you have to know how to use them. Take the time to discover, understand, and analyze them. Feel free to ask for help when needed. YouTube is full of useful videos.

3. DOMAIN NAMES

Domain name registries often suggest available domain names, similar to the one you want. This can give you ideas for your company name.

5.2 - THE 5 STEPS OF THE PROCESS

Here are the five steps in the process that should help you find the right name for your company. To illustrate this process, I will tell you the story behind the name of my company CorpoMax Inc.

1. FIND THE KEYWORDS

The first step is to find relevant keywords. First and foremost, you need to make a complete list of them:

- Keywords specific to your sector of activity
- Keywords specific to the services or products you will offer
- Keywords specific to the elements that will distinguish you from the competition
- Keywords in the language of the markets you want to enter

In 2001, I decided to launch a company specializing in the creation of American companies throughout the United States.

First, I drew up a list of keywords specific to this industry:

- America
- Binder
- Business
- Bylaws
- Company
- Corporate
- Corporation
- Delaware
- Head Office
- Incorporation
- Law
- Ledger
- Limited liability company
- LLC
- Minutes
- Operating Agreement
- Seal
- State
- United States
- USA

Given my desire to offer services to French-speaking people as well as to English-speaking people, I also prepared a list of keywords in French:

- Affaires
- Amérique
- Classeur
- Compagnie
- Constitution
- Convention d'opération
- Corporatif
- Corporation
- Création
- État

- États-Unis
- Incorporation
- Livre
- Loi
- Procès-verbal
- Règlements
- Résolution
- Responsabilité limitée
- Siège social
- Société
- Sceau
- Tampon

Finally, I found some keywords related to the distinctive elements I wanted to offer to my future clientele:

- Advice
- Family business
- Listening
- Maximum
- Professional
- Quality
- Reliability
- Service
- Speed
- Trust

2. ANALYZE THE COMPETITION

The second step is to analyze the competition. Before choosing the name of your company, it is important to explore the competitive environment in which it will evolve. This allows you to discover the names of your future competitors and ensure that your company name will be distinctive.

Analyzing does not mean copying. On the contrary, you must do everything possible to distinguish yourself from the competition. That is what Sir Richard Branson did when he founded Virgin Airlines. He chose this name brilliantly for his new company, allowing him to immediately distinguish himself from other airlines, whose names were always linked to their geographical origin - American Airlines, Air France, Air Canada, etc.

In the case of CorpoMax, I analyzed the websites of more than 150 direct competitors, not to mention the countless law firms, certified public accountants, and tax experts across the United States. This allowed me to analyze their names and ensure that the name of my company would be distinctive. My credibility was at stake, not only in the eyes of my future customers, but also in the eyes of my future competitors. It would have been inappropriate and unperceived for my new company to be sued in court for choosing a name similar to that of a well-established company. Respect attracts respect.

3. USE THE TOOLS

The third step is to use the tools. I repeat: take the time to discover all the tools at your disposal. Just like building a house, choosing your company name is not just a matter of minutes. You need to take the time to discover your tools and learn how to use them. Only then can you use them intelligently.

In the case of CorpoMax, I used all the tools at my disposal:

- The Google search engine
- The dictionaries
- The rare social networks that existed at the time
- The business registry of the state of Delaware, the ideal place to create an American company
- The trademark registers in the United States, Canada, the European Community, and Switzerland
- The domain name registers, my favorite being GoDaddy.

Next, I analyzed the keywords and played with them, visually and audibly.

Finally, I wanted to find a name that could be easily pronounced in both English and French.

4. CONSULT YOUR RELATIVES

The fourth step is to consult your family and friends. Once you have found the right company name, it is time to share with the people you trust:

- Parents
- Friends
- Colleagues

Do not do it until you find THE name. Do not present ten names. At the end of the day, you will have to make a choice, not them. If you hesitate between two names only, you can then ask for their opinion.

But be careful! Remember the following three rules:

Rule no. 1: Only consult people who are absolutely trustworthy, whether or not they are part of your family or circle of friends.

Rule no. 2: Analyze all of their comments and suggestions quietly, without taking an immediate decision. When it comes to finding the right name for your company, time is often your best ally.

Rule no. 3: Believe deeply in the power of your subconscious. It is often a neglected or misunderstood tool. It is free, it works 24 hours a day, and it is particularly powerful during your sleep.

In the case of CorpoMax, I consulted my immediate family and two close friends, to whom I submitted only the current name of my company. As you may have guessed, *CorpoMax* is the union of *Corpo* (for Corporation) and *Max* (for Maximum).

5. MAKE A DECISION

The fifth and final step is to make a decision. Finally, decide. Make a decision. Not easy, but it has to be. Analyze, but get it done. In English, we say: *Analysis, paralysis*. Indeed, too much analysis paralyses. You will not be able to please everyone. Anyway, that is not your goal. In the end, you make the decision, no one else. Make your decision without undue influence. Ultimately, it is you, your customers, your employees, and your professional environment that will live with your company name. Not your family, friends, or colleagues. In the case of CorpoMax, I chose this name after having analyzed and checked everything:

- Length of name: OK, because only three syllables
- Spelling of name: OK, because easy to write
- Pronunciation of name: OK for both clienteles
- Meaning of name: OK, because made-up word
- Sound of name: OK in both languages
- Appearance of name: OK for the company name and domain name.
- Originality of name: OK, because distinctive from my competitors' names

Two weeks after starting the research process, I made my decision. Today, almost twenty years later, I still find my company name just as beautiful as ever!

Finally, here are three points you should remember.

1. PASSION

Live passionately looking for the name of your company. This is a crucial step in its establishment and an exciting time in your professional life.

2. DISCRETION

Be absolutely discreet. Do not share your company name and domain name ideas on the web. Stay discreet in public places—restaurants, waiting rooms, etc. Good ideas can be stolen anywhere, by anyone.

3. SANDWICHES

In 1972, two brothers living in New Jersey launched a modest sandwich restaurant they called *The Sub Shop.* In 1975, the restaurant's accountant bought it. He thought the restaurant's name was not distinctive. So, he organized a contest in the community to see who could come up with a new name. After receiving more than 10,000 proposals, he chose *Port of Subs.* At the time, this type of contest was probably an interesting idea, because the Internet did not exist. Today, the same contest would undoubtedly attract several cybersquatters, preventing the restaurant from easily registering its domain name.

5.3 - THE 3 URBAN LEGENDS

When looking for the name of your company, you may read or hear pessimistic or even negative comments. Some of them will even mention urban legends. Here are three of them.

1. THE NAME OF YOUR COMPANY IS NOT THAT IMPORTANT.

That is not true.

The name of your company is crucial!

If you do not follow the process of research, analysis, and decision making, you will regret it bitterly.

One day, not so long ahead, you will have to face the facts. At that time, it will be expensive to change your company name.

The only exception to this is the name of a holding company that will have no contact with customers. In such a case, a numerical or unattractive name may generally be sufficient.

2. NO INTERESTING NAMES ARE AVAILABLE.

That is not true.

There are thousands of company names waiting to be discovered. To do this, you must follow the research, analysis, and decision-making process described previously.

The availability problem is not so much on the side of the company name as on the side of its domain name.

This is why it is often better for you to create your company name, rather than using common words. This will have the advantage of adding a distinctive touch to your company name and making it easier to obtain its domain name.

3. THE NAME MUST BE DESCRIPTIVE TO HELP SEARCH ENGINES.

That is not true.

The science behind the algorithms used by the search engines is opaque. Google has never revealed the elements of its science, all of which is a very well protected trade secret.

Some argue that the use of descriptive words in a company or domain name can indeed facilitate the position of your website in the ranking of search results.

If this theory is correct, it means that several known sites are very low in such a ranking:

- amazon.com
- apple.com
- hp.com
- microsoft.com

Keywords describing your company's products or services should not be part of your company name, but rather part of its website.

. . .

Finally, here are three points you should remember.

1. INFLUENCE

In business, you should not be guided or influenced by urban legends. Even less so when it comes to finding the name of your company.

2. SPECIALIST

If you are really stuck in the process of creating your company name, consider hiring a firm specialized in the field.

3. YOUR INSTINCT

History has shown that sometimes certain company names become popular even if they do not meet the traditional selection criteria. For example, who would have thought that Amazon, Apple, and Yahoo! would become household names. In other words, consider my suggestions, but ultimately follow your entrepreneurial instinct.

5.4 - THE 5 MISTAKES NOT TO MAKE

In life, we make mistakes. However, our ultimate goal is to make as little as possible. Here are five mistakes to avoid during the process of searching for your company name.

1. INVOLVING TOO MANY PEOPLE IN CHOOSING YOUR COMPANY NAME

There is proof that a business name that is chosen by consensus often gives mixed results. The name chosen by a group, or by a majority of members of a group, generally lacks flavor and is referred to as a *vanilla name*.

2. ORGANIZING A PUBLIC CONTEST TO FIND YOUR COMPANY NAME

You will receive several names, have to make a choice and give a prize. But what happens if none of the submitted names satisfy you?

3 FAILING TO CHECK THE MEANING OF THE NAME IN SEVERAL LANGUAGES

Even if you have a local vision for now, be open-minded. Plan instead of regret.

4. CHOOSING YOUR COMPANY NAME REGARDLESS OF THE AVAILABILITY OF THE DOMAIN NAME

Today, one of the first instincts of your potential customers is to go to your company's website. What will they think if the domain name they assume belongs to a company other than yours?

5. FAILING TO FILE A TRADEMARK APPLICATION

The name of a company does not equate to a trademark, at least at the legal level. Remember to apply for registration of your trademark, in connection with the products or services you offer.

Finally, here are three points you should remember.

1. SIXTH MISTAKE

A sixth mistake is to refuse to change a bad name. If your company has a name that is not—or no longer—adequate, do not resist the change and find another name. Yes, it will be painful. No, it will not be easy. But, in the end, you will correct the situation and your company will reap the benefits.

2. TIME

Take the time required to choose the name of your company. In this area, speed is a poor advisor. Reflection must always precede action.

3. CORPOMAX

In April 2001, it took me two weeks to finally decide on the name *CorpoMax*. Today, almost twenty years later, I still love the name as much as ever. I think it has aged well. And I am convinced that in twenty years' time, it will still be as beautiful - at least in my eyes!

5.5 - THE 20 TYPES OF NAMES TO AVOID

Not all company names are born equal. Here are 20 types of company names that you should not use.

1. GENERAL NAME

The first type of name to avoid is a general name. This type of name has no distinctive character. Not today, not tomorrow.

- Bakery Products Inc.
- International Business Machines (fortunately now IBM)

Here are a few words which generally do not - or no longer - belong in a company name:

- Advantage
- Agency
- Business
- Company
- Global
- Group

- Industry
- International
- Network
- Overseas
- Products
- Professional
- Services
- Strategic
- Solutions
- Systems
- Universal
- Worldwide

It is essential that your company be able to differentiate itself from its competitors. It starts with its name.

2. OLD FORM NAME

The second type of name to avoid is an old form name. Here are some examples:

- Allard Enterprises
- Cocorico Partners
- CorpoMax & Co.
- Gogopro Group

Learn from the past, live in the present, think of the future. So name your company accordingly.

3. NAME WITH A TROUBLED PAST

The third type of name to avoid is a name with a troubled past. If you choose the name of a company that has gone bankrupt or closed in disgrace, it may not be your best decision as an entrepreneur. One day, collective memory can catch up with you, especially because of the Internet.

Here are some examples of well-known companies in the United States that have had to close their doors:

- Blockbusters
- Enron
- Weinstein Company

If the name of a bankrupt company has a certain value in your eyes, it is better to use a different legal identifier, to reduce the risk of confusion:

- Old company > ABC Inc.
- New company > ABC Corp.

It is also possible to insert the incorporation date in the name:

- Old company > ABC Inc.
- New company > ABC (2020) Inc.

4. NAME BANNED BY SEARCH ENGINES

The fourth type of name to avoid is a name banned by search engines. Google has a strict policy regarding domain names used to send junk or spam, commit fraud, or spread malware. It is therefore recommended to do some research on the coveted name before adopting it.

5. NAME WITH A SHORTENED WORD

The fifth type of name to avoid is a name with a shortened word. Here are some examples of shortened words:

- Intl - instead of International

- Mktg - instead of Marketing

Before choosing this type of name, ask yourself two questions:

- First, are you sending a text message or SMS to your friend?
- Second, how will you communicate your company's name, over the phone or in person?

6. NAME ATTRACTING TOO MUCH ATTENTION

The sixth type of name to avoid is a name that attracts too much attention.

Some company names may be of interest to tax authorities:

- Tax Exempt Offshore

Other names may scare off banks:

- New York Pornstars

7. NOT SERIOUS NAME

The seventh type of name to avoid is an unserious name. Humor has no place in every industry. For example, you are targeting a clientele made up of multinationals operating in the aeronautics industry. If you name your company *Hakuna Matata Inc.*, it is probably better to review your plans and open a daycare center instead.

In short, what you need to keep in mind is how others will perceive your company. In this context, your own perception is much less important.

8. TRENDY NAME

The eighth type of name to avoid is a trendy name. ABC Namebank claims that following the advent of Google - shortly preceded by Wanadoo in France - nearly 800 companies have adopted a name with the double O. Trends also hit some new names, which have a spelling anomaly:

- Flickr
- Grindr
- Tumblr

By definition, fashion is fleeting. On the contrary, the name of your company must be immutable, timeless.

9. OFFENSIVE NAME

The ninth type of name to avoid is an offensive name. The name of a company sometimes includes a word that may offend a particular segment of the population. For example, the name of the *Washington Redskins* football team refers to the color of the skin of indigenous people. This leads to regular calls to boycott this sports team and its products. Obviously, it is better to adopt a company name that does not offend anyone.

10. HATED NAME

The tenth type of name to avoid is a hated name. Here are some examples of words you should not include in your company name:

- Daesh
- Isis

Some companies have even had to change their company or brand names because of the high profile of this terrorist group. For example, the *Isis Wallet* mobile payment service has decided to change its name to *Softcard.*

11. CONFUSING NAME

The eleventh type of name to avoid is a confusing name. It is important to avoid at all costs choosing a company name that is confusing with:

- The name of an existing company
- The name of a competitor
- The name of a brand
- The name of a government agency
- A distinctive domain name

Note that confusion can be visual as well as audible.

The risk of confusion must be minimized, as the consequences can be negative. Several risks arise from the confusion. Here are some of them:

- Commercial Risk > Confusion in the minds of consumers
- Legal Risk > Lawsuits
- Media Risk > Negative reactions in traditional and social media
- Financial Risk > Legal fees, damages, name change costs

It is simple: if the company name you choose may create confusion with an existing company or brand name, choose another name.

12. TECHNOLOGY-RELATED NAME

The twelfth type of name to avoid is a name linked to a technology. Please do not choose a name that contains a technological reference. Technology is like fashion: it changes quickly! Coincidentally or not, the Canadian mobile phone operator *Bell Cellular* had to quickly change its name to *Bell Mobility*.

13. NAME WITH A MONETARY CONNOTATION

The thirteenth type of name to avoid is a name with a monetary connotation. It is strongly recommended not to use words that refer to money in your company name. Here are some words to suggest financial management of money belonging to or coming from third parties:

- Asset Management
- Capital
- Credit
- Equity
- Finance
- Investment
- Loan
- Money
- Mortgage
- Savings
- Trade

Of course, derivatives of these words should also be avoided:

- Invest
- Trader, Trading

A company name with a reference to money or the management of other people's money will cause you problems when you try to open a bank account. Banks want to be the only ones to manage other people's money. However, nothing prevents you from specifying the nature of your activities under your company name, rather than within it.

14. RESTRICTED NAME

The fourteenth type of name to avoid is a restricted name. As a general rule, your company cannot suggest, without prior authorization from a regulatory body:

- That it is a government agency, a financial institution, an insurance company, or a police force;
- That it carries on activities regulated by a professional association.

There are words whose use is controlled by government authorities:

- Bank
- Federal
- Government
- Insurance
- Police
- School
- Trust

Other words see their use controlled by professional associations:

- Architects
- Attorneys
- Engineers
- Etc.

Of course, derivatives of these words are also subject to control:

- Banker, Banking

In the United States, in addition to the federal government, there are 50 states and the District of Columbia, not to mention the hundreds of professional associations in each state. Therefore, there are thousands of rules concerning restricted words. What is allowed in one state may well be prohibited in another. When you wish to use a restricted word in your company name, a proper application must first be filed with the appropriate organization:

- Generally, the request for derogation is quite long and tedious to complete.
- The time it takes to review your application varies from one organization to another.
- There is no guarantee that your application will be accepted.
- If your application is accepted, special conditions may apply.

15. SOCIALLY UNACCEPTABLE NAME

The fifteenth type of name to avoid is a socially unacceptable name. In the United States, each state has its own rules regarding business names. A company name with one or more socially unacceptable words will be rejected:

- By government authorities
- By society in general.

Socially unacceptable words include words with a connotation that is:

- Crude
- Discriminatory
- Immoral
- Obscene
- Racist
- Scandalous
- Sexual
- Violent

A socially acceptable word in your language may have a completely unacceptable connotation in another. This is why it is crucial to check the meaning of your company name in several languages.

16. DESCRIPTIVE NAME

The sixteenth type of name to avoid is a descriptive name. This type of name is not memorable. Imagine if *Amazon* was called *General Store*…

If you have a generic domain name, such as *Bicycles.com*:

- The company name *Bicycles Inc.* will be descriptive.
- The company name *Bicycles.com Inc.* will be a little more distinctive.

17. NAME OF INDIVIDUAL

The seventeenth type of name to avoid is an individual's name. Today, personalizing a company name is rarely a good idea. This is even more true when the company name contains not only the family name, but also the first name of its founder:

- John Smith Renovation Center

When John passes away, what will his estate do with the name of the company?

18. GEOGRAPHIC NAME

The eighteenth type of name to avoid is a geographic name. To specify means to restrict. It is best not to unnecessarily limit the perception that your potential customers may have about the geographical scope of your company's activities. Indeed, they may think that the service is provided in that city or region only. Moreover, some companies have changed their names, in particular to remove any geographic reference:

- Kentucky Fried Chicken > KFC
- Minnesota Manufacturing and Mining > 3M

On the other hand, a company that wishes to offer services locally will undoubtedly have an interest in specifying its geographic location in its name:

- Boston Plumbing
- Brooklyn Electric

19. TEMPORAL NAME

The nineteenth type of name to avoid is a name with a temporal reference. Any reference to time in your company name is risky:

- Sport Shoes 2000

20. NAME OF A PRODUCT OR SERVICE

Finally, the twentieth type of name to avoid is the name of a product or service. If your company is named after its first or most popular product, this can sometimes be a problem. But sometimes it is not. In general, it is better for your company to have its own name, separate from that of its products or services. Here are some examples of companies that have adopted the name of their main product or service:

- Research in Motion > BlackBerry
- Evenflow > DropBox
- Relational Software > Oracle
- Tokyo Telecommunications Engineering > Sony

Finally, here are three points you should remember.

1. BANK

Although a company name is legally acceptable, this does not mean that it will be acceptable to your bank. If you wish to open a bank account for your company, the bank compliance department may refuse to open it for various reasons. One of these is the content or meaning of your company name.

2. CIRCUMSTANCES

Sometimes, circumstances or opportunities mean that you may have to choose a name theoretically to avoid. Never forget that any good rule is generally subject to exceptions.

3. LAST NAME

It may sometimes be acceptable or even appropriate for a company to have the family name of its founder. If this is your case, avoid inserting your first name in your company name. Your estate will be eternally grateful to you.

5.6 - 25 FAMOUS NAMES: WHERE DO THEY COME FROM?

Every day, we are in contact - voluntarily or not - with company and brand names. Knowing the origin of 25 of them may perhaps provide you with some inspiration.

1. ADIDAS

Name forged from the name of its founder, Adolf (Adi) Dassler.

2. ADOBE

Name of the stream behind the house of co-founder John Warnock.

3. APPLE

Favorite fruit of co-founder Steve Jobs.

4. COCA-COLA

Name forged from coca leaves and kola nuts.

5. DANONE – DANNON IN THE UNITED STATES

Name forged from the nickname of Daniel, first son of the founder Isaac Carasso (Dan-one).

6. DHL

Initials of the last name of the three founders — Adrian Dalsey, Larry Hillblom, and Robert Lynn.

7. EBAY

Owner of Echo Bay Technology Group, its founder Pierre Omidyar wished to reserve the domain name echobay.com. Given its unavailability, he chose ebay.com.

8. ESSO

Pronunciation of the initials S and O, of the words Standard Oil.

9. GOOGLE

Spelling error — intended or not — of the word *googol*, which represents a number starting with 1 and followed by 100 zeros.

10. IKEA

Name made up of the initials of the name of its founder — Ingvar Kamprad —, of his parents' farm — Elmtaryd — and of the village where he was born — Agunnaryd, Sweden.

11. INTEL

Name forged from the words Integrated Electronics.

12. KEURIG

Dutch word meaning *neat.*

13. MATTEL

Name forged from the first name of the founders Harold (Matt) Matson and Elliot Handler.

14. NIKE

Name of the goddess of victory in Greek mythology.

15. NIKON

Name forged from the words *Nippon Kogaru* which mean *Japanese optics.*

16. PEPSI

Name derived from the digestive enzyme *pepsin.*

17. REEBOK

Name in Afrikaans of the gray rhebok, a type of African antelope.

18. SAMSONITE

Name derived from the biblical character Samson, known for his strength.

19. SKYPE

The starting concept used the words *Sky Peer to Peer*. Everything was shortened to become *Skyper*, and finally *Skype*.

20. SONY

Name derived from the Latin word *sonus*, which means *sound*, and the American word *sonny*, which the Japanese used in order to mean *brilliant youngster.*

21. STARBUCKS

Name inspired by the character of *Starbuck*, in the book *Moby-Dick or The Whale*, written in 1851 by the American author Herman Melville.

22. TEXACO

Name derived from *The Texas Company U.S.S.*

23. VOLKSWAGEN

Name meaning *people's car* in German.

24. VOLVO

Word meaning *I roll* in Latin.

25. XEROX

Name derived from the word *xerography*, itself derived from the Greek words *xeros* — dry — and *graphos* — write.

6 - HOW TO PROTECT YOUR BUSINESS NAME

6.1 - PROTECTION NO. 1: BUSINESS NAME

The first level of protection for your business name is related to its use.

You must use the name consistently.

For example, if your company name consists of two distinct words - which are not stuck together, you must write and display them separately at all times:

- Advertising
- Business cards
- Documentation
- Invoices
- Letterheads
- Statements
- Website
- Etc.

INCONSISTENT USE

Above all, your graphic designer must not be allowed to change the name of your company:

- By pasting two separate words
- By splitting a one-word name on two lines

Here are some examples of inconsistent use:

- Bob & Bobette | Bob&Bobette | Bob and Bobette
- MacDonald | Mac Donald | McDonald | Mc Donald
- The Wall Street Journal | Wall Street Journal | WSJ

Also, a name that is too long always leads to a shortened use by your customers, suppliers, employees, and yourself:

- Business Worldwide Enterprises > BWE
- Diamond Global Ventures > DGV

Again, this should convince you to choose a short name.

Finally, here are three points you should remember.

1. WORDS STUCK TOGETHER

The fashion for pasted words comes mainly from the global invasion of domain names. Do not let this trend dilute or change your company's real name.

2. HOLDING

If your company is a holding company, a uniform use of its name may be a little less important, as there is usually no interaction with the public.

Nevertheless, get into the habit of calling a spade a spade. This way, when you need to sign a contract on behalf of your holding company, you can remember its exact name.

3. SPELLING

To ensure that everyone uses your company name consistently, make sure that its spelling is normal:

- Razr > Razor

6.2 - PROTECTION NO. 2: DOMAIN NAME

The second level of protection for your company name comes from the reservation of its domain name. The choice of your company name and the choice of its primary domain name are intrinsically linked. Today, you can no longer choose a company name without checking at the same time the availability of the domain name.

CHARACTERISTICS OF THE DOMAIN NAME

The characteristics of the domain name are identical to those of your company name. Indeed, your domain name:

- Must be short
- Must be easy to write and easy to spell
- Must have a meaning that is easy to understand
- Must be easy to pronounce
- Must have a pleasant sound
- Must have a pleasant visual appearance
- Must be unique, memorable, and attractive.

WHICH DOMAIN NAME TO CHOOSE?

But which domain name should you choose? Despite the multiplicity of extensions available on the market, the domain name to choose is ideally the one ending with the .com extension. This is the best known and most popular extension in the world.

THE .NET EXTENSION

If the .com extension is not available, but the .net extension is, do not choose it:

- The natural instinct of consumers is to use the .com extension.
- If you choose the .net extension for not being able to get its .com colleague, the risk of confusion in the minds of your potential customers will be permanent.

A riskier strategy is to still choose the .net domain name and wait for the .com to become available. But the risk is big:

- The .com name may never become available.
- When it becomes available, its owner will be aware of the existence of your .net domain name, allowing them to request an inflated purchase price.
- In addition, what will be the history of the coveted domain name? Will it have been subjected to Google's wrath for prohibited practices?
- During all this time, confusion will reign in the minds of your potential customers.

ACTION WORD

Another strategy is to choose a domain name that includes your company name and add an action word:

By adding a prefix

- get: getdropbox.com - which became dropbox.com
- go: goharrisjewelry.com
- hello: hellosmithgarage.com
- my: mycoffee.com

By adding a suffix

- online: coffeeonline.com

FIELD OF ACTIVITY

Another strategy is to choose a domain name that has an extension specific to your field of activity. Here is a partial list of descriptive extensions:

- .app
- .business
- .cafe
- .cloud
- .club
- .expert
- .kitchen
- .media
- .photography
- .pizza
- .restaurant
- .salon
- .science
- .shop
- .sport
- .store
- .tech
- .training

GEOGRAPHIC EXTENSION

Another strategy is to choose a domain name with a geographic extension. Some are very well established in the minds of consumers. For example, domain names ending in .ca and .fr resonate positively in the minds of Canadian and French residents. However, this is not the case in the United States, where the .us extension is not very popular.

WORLDWIDE

If you have international plans, it is better to choose a .com domain name or a descriptive extension. Later on, you will be able to reserve country-specific domain names:

- Where your company will be located
- Where your company will do business

CORRELATION REQUIRED

In most cases, the domain name and your company name should be identical. Indeed, experts agree that Google attaches great importance to the correlation between the two names. It is logical that this correlation should also be made in the minds of your potential customers. For example, if your company name is *Abbar Furniture*, its domain name should be *AbbarFurniture.com* and not *AFurniture.com*.

HOW MANY DOMAIN NAMES?

When you start the process of choosing your company name, you must at the same time check the availability of its domain name.

The rules to follow are simple:

- Make sure to choose a .com domain name or, if not available, a domain name with a descriptive or geographic extension.

- Reserve at least ten domain names with various extensions, as a defensive measure.
- Redirect all or part of these domain names to your main one. For example, if visitors indicate *gogopro.net* in the address bar of their browser, they will see the *gogopro.com* site appear.

DERIVATIVE OR SIMILAR DOMAIN NAMES

In addition to the primary domain name you have chosen, you should also reserve derivative or similar domain names, including those with a typographical error.

Several large companies have done so:

Amazon

- amaxon.com
- amazzon.com
- ammazon.com
- ammazzon.com
- amazone.com

Facebook

- facebok.com
- facbook.com
- faceboook.com
- faceobok.com

Google

- gooogle.com
- gogle.com
- gogole.com
- google.net
- goolge.com

- googel.com
- googl.com
- googlr.com
- g00gle.com
- googlee.com
- googil.com
- ggoogle.com
- gewgol.com
- gewgle.com
- googlecom.com

SHORTENED DOMAIN NAMES

You can also reserve a shortened version of your domain name.

The logic applicable to domain names is exactly the same as that applicable to company names: shorter is better.

Amazon

- amzn.to

American Airlines

- aa.com

Facebook

- fb.com
- fb.me
- i.org

Hewlett-Packard

- hpe.com
- hp.com

LinkedIn

- linked.in

Messenger

- m.me

Pitney Bowes

- pb.com

Wall Street Journal

- wsj.com

Weight Watchers

- ww.com

NEGATIVE DOMAIN NAMES

As a preventive measure, you can also acquire negative domain names, as Facebook does on a regular basis:

- AboutFacebook.com
- Facebook.adult
- FacebookCheats.com
- FacebookCreditsSuck.org
- FBCreditsSuck.org
- IHateFacebookCredits.com
- IHateTheFacebookLikeButton.com
- KillFacebook.com
- LikeButtonSucks.com
- LikeSucks.com

Several large American companies reserve domain names that may damage their image, but often anonymously.

IN WHOSE NAME?

Domain names can be registered:

- In the name of your company
- In your own name
- In the name of your holding company

Domain names should absolutely not be registered:

- In the name of your employee
- In the name of your webmaster
- In the name of your distributor

CONTROL OVER DOMAIN NAMES

You must have exclusive - or at least shared - access to the control center for your domain names, provided by your registrar. Many horror stories stem from giving employees or webmasters exclusive access to the company's domain name control center.

ACQUISITION OF AN EXISTING DOMAIN NAME

If you have chosen the perfect name for your company, but the domain name is not available, there may be a solution. Since the popularity of the Internet exploded, millions of people around the world have sniffed out the economic potential of owning domain names for subsequent resale. Therefore, there is a whole industry that has developed around the resale of domain names:

- Some domain names are sold by their owner, without outside help. In such a case, there is a high risk of fraud. Your

recourse against the fraudster, if any, can be complex, expensive, and risky.
- Other domain names are sold online, through a specialized firm, at a fixed price or by auction.
- Finally, several sites offer expired domain names for sale.

In 2011, Apple paid more than $5 million to acquire the domain name *icloud.com.* In 2015, Apple acquired 170 domain names containing the word *iCloud.*

TOOLS

In the United States, there are several domain name registrars. Their websites usually include a powerful search tool, which offers several alternatives when the desired domain name is not available.

Finally, here are three points you should remember.

1. B&H PHOTO

B&H Photo, a New York store specializing in the sale of photo, video, and audio equipment, has nearly 500 domain names, the majority of which are redirected to the main domain *bhphotovideo.com.* For its part, Google has over 3,000 domain names while Facebook holds more than 3,500.

2. SILENCE!

Do not broadcast your company name until you have reserved its main domain name and derived domain names. Otherwise, cybersquatters will be happy to make you regret it. This is what happened to Yahoo! in early 2017 when the company decided to change its name to *Altaba,* following the sale of several assets. When the change was announced,

Yahoo! had only registered the domain name *altaba.com*. In just a few hours, cybersquatters have acquired dozens of *altaba* domain names with various extensions.

3. FACEBOOK

When he launched Facebook, Mark Zuckerberg registered the domain name *thefacebook.com* — including the empty word *the*. He quickly realized that *shorter is better*. In 2005, he bought the domain name *facebook.com* for $200,000. Then, he reserved nearly 2,000 domain names that are derived from the word Facebook. Finally, in 2010, Facebook acquired the domain name *fb.com* for the modest sum of $8.5 million.

6.3 - PROTECTION NO. 3: TRADEMARK

The third level of protection for your company name is related to the filing of a trademark application. This is an important additional protection. Indeed, more than one company may have the same name in the United States, considering that each of the 50 states - as well as the District of Columbia - has jurisdiction to establish legal entities.

To ensure that you obtain exclusivity in the use of your company name in relation to specific products or services, filing a trademark application is often recommended. It is important to act quickly. The protection of your intellectual property is of paramount importance. Too often, entrepreneurs fail to file an application for registration of their trademark, which sometimes leads to deplorable situations.

OBJECT OF THE TRADEMARK

A trademark may be registered in relation to:

- Products
- Services

IN WHOSE NAME?

A trademark can be registered:

- In the name of your company
- In your own name
- In the name of your holding company

Above all, a trademark must not be registered:

- In the name of your employee
- In the name of your consultant
- In the name of your distributor

ORGANIZATIONS

The United States Patent and Trademark Office - USPTO - is responsible for the trademark register. It is recommended to register your trademark in the country or countries where you plan to do business.

INTERNATIONAL APPLICATION

Some international treaties make it possible to file an international trademark application, such as:

- Madrid Agreement - 1891
- Protocol relating to the Madrid Agreement — 1989

An intellectual property lawyer will be able to advise you in this regard.

Finally, here are three points you should remember.

1. NOT REGISTRABLE

If your trademark is descriptive, it will generally not be registered. For example, it would not be possible to protect the brand *BIG TV* in connection with televisions. In addition, if your trademark is likely to cause confusion with an existing trademark, it cannot be registered.

2. LAWYER

Do not make the mistake of filing an application for registration of your trademark yourself. Hire a lawyer who specializes in intellectual property law. Otherwise, you may regret it, especially when you receive a first report from the government examiner, asking you to answer legal questions. In any case, since August 3, 2019, any foreign person - natural or legal - who wishes to register a trademark in the United States must be represented by an American lawyer.

3. PRODUCTS

Consider registering a trademark not only in relation to the services offered by your company, but also to the products it offers. For example, Apple has registered not only the Apple trademark, but also the following:

- AirPods
- HomePod
- iMac
- iPad
- iPhone
- iPod
- MacBook
- MacBook Air
- MacBook Pro
- Mac Pro
- Etc.

6.4 - PROTECTION NO. 4: SOCIAL NETWORKS

The fourth level of protection for your company name is its registration on social networks. The main social networks to consider to date are the following:

- Facebook
- Instagram
- LinkedIn
- Pinterest
- Reddit
- Snapchat
- TikTok
- Tumblr
- Twitter
- Vimeo
- YouTube

SEVERAL SOCIAL NETWORKS

You should subscribe to as many social networks as possible, even if you do not plan to use them all. At least two reasons justify this approach.

First, by subscribing to the main social networks, you often get a username - social media handle - corresponding to your company name:

- facebook.com/corpomax
- youtube.com/corpomax
- twitter.com/corpomax
- linkedin.com/company/corpomax

Second, if you fail to register on one of the major social networks, it may allow others to do so before you. Sometimes with unexpected consequences:

- instagram.com/corpomax

USERNAME

If the username you want is not available, be creative. If your company name consists of two words, insert a period between them:

- If *BlueConsulting* is not available, maybe *Blue.Consulting* will be.

Be consistent on all social networks on which you have chosen to register your company. The same username, logo, and color palette should be used to show that your company is unique.

~

Finally, here are three points you should remember.

1. SHORT USERNAME

Choose a username of 15 characters or less. Some social networks accept a longer username, but it makes sense to adopt the same username for all social networks. This further reinforces my initial recommendation: choose a short company name!

2. WEB TOOLS

In the *Useful Resources* section, you will find a list of web tools to help you find the right username.

3. DICTOMAX

In 2016, I decided to start a fourth company, offering online training for entrepreneurs and professionals. After a few weeks, I found the name *DictoMax*. I made sure the name of my new company was available in the State of Delaware, as well as in the trademark register in the United States, Canada, European Community, and Switzerland. I also made sure the username *dictomax* was available on various social networks. However, I forgot to check... Twitter.

A little later, I discovered that someone on Twitter had the username *@dictomax*. However, I noticed that this user was not active, was following only a few people or celebrities, and had hardly any followers. I also guessed that this person lived in the province of Québec, where I come from. I therefore hired an investigation agency and gave it the difficult task of identifying the owner of this Twitter account. Two weeks later, the agency gave me the name and address of the person in question.

So I contacted this person and explained that I had just started a business. All it was missing was a Twitter account under its own name. Thankfully, the person was kind enough to agree to transfer her Twitter account to me. In return, I gave her a check with a donation of $250 to a charity of her choice. Very lucky, I was...

6.5 - PROTECTION NO. 5: SEARCH ENGINES

The fifth level of protection for your company name is its registration on the main business search engines:

- Bing Places for Business
- Google My Business
- Yahoo! Small Business

ADVANTAGES

Registering your business with these search engines offers several advantages.

First, registration formalizes the existence of your business on each of these search engines by allowing you to create a business profile.

Second, registration allows you to provide useful information to your potential customers, including:

- The name of your business
- Its logo
- Its physical address

- Its main email address
- Its telephone number
- Its website address
- Opening hours, if applicable
- Photos that you have posted

Third, registration provides visibility for your business in at least two places on Google's search engine:

- Google Search
- Google Maps

Fourth, registration allows Internet users to post questions, comments, and suggestions.

Finally, registration allows Internet users to send you messages and allows you to reply to them.

DISADVANTAGES

Registering your business on these search engines still has a significant disadvantage. Indeed, some individuals may post unflattering or even untruthful comments on your company profile. In such a case, always respond in a courteous manner and invite them to contact you to discuss their grievances.

Finally, here are three points you should remember.

1. FREE

Do not wait to register your new company on the major search engines. It is free and can only help your business stand out from the crowd.

2. NEGLIGENCE

If you neglect these registrations, a malicious third party may do so on your behalf, with inaccurate or misleading information. It will then be more difficult for you to claim your *digital* property rights from Google, Bing, and Yahoo!

3. ADVERTISING TOOLS

Do not underestimate the effectiveness of the advertising tools offered by the main search engines:

- Amazon Advertising
- Bing Ads
- Google Ads

Of course, it will cost you a few dollars. But quality, well-targeted advertising can generally provide you with significant benefits.

6.6 - ACT ALONE VS. HIRE AN EXPERT

Today, it is becoming easier to do things that were once reserved for specialists. The development of the Internet has allowed people to easily and quickly enrich and share their knowledge. When it comes to finding the name of your company, you have a choice:

- Do the whole process yourself
- Entrust the task to an expert

ADVANTAGES OF HIRING AN EXPERT

There are three advantages to hiring a specialist:

- First, you immediately benefit from the expert's knowledge and experience.
- Second, you immediately benefit from the mastery of the tools by this expert.
- Finally, you can focus on creating and launching your business.

DISADVANTAGES OF HIRING AN EXPERT

However, there are at least two significant disadvantages:

- First, the cost of the expert's services can sometimes be quite high. It often varies between $5,000 and $100,000.
- Second, your active participation will still be solicited by the expert in the name search process.

That is why it is often better to choose the name of your business yourself. It is your baby, an intangible being to whom you will give life. After using the tools discussed previously, you should be able to find the ideal name for your business.

~

Now, let us analyze your needs for the five levels of protection we discussed earlier.

1. COMPANY NAME

The first level of protection concerns the use of your company name. You generally do not need an expert at this level. It is about using common sense and following my recommendations.

Of course, you can hire a graphic designer to create your brand image, your logo, and your website. But, under no circumstances, should the graphic designer take control of your company name, whose uniformity of use is crucial. In this respect, you must be the only decider.

- If your graphic designer suggests that you put your company name on two lines, when it is a single word, say no.
- If your graphic designer suggests you stick the two words of your business name together, say no.

I repeat: use your company name consistently everywhere.

2. DOMAIN NAME

The second level of protection concerns the registration of a domain name. Again, you do not need an expert to register a domain name. This process takes only five minutes.

However, do not make the mistake of entrusting the task of registering your domain name to a third party, for example a webmaster or an employee you do not trust perfectly. How many times have I seen a domain name registered in favor of the webmaster or employee, instead of the company? You alone or a very small group of people must have access to the customer area on the registrar's website for your domain name.

However, it may be interesting to retain the services of a web research specialist. With the help of well-chosen keywords, this expert will be able to help position your website favorably on search engines.

3. TRADEMARK

The third level of protection concerns the filing of a trademark. In theory, you can apply for a trademark registration yourself. In practice, you will make a mistake. Although this may seem easy, the filing of a trademark must be preceded by:

- A serious analysis of your current and potential needs
- The preparation of a precise list of the products or services concerned by the trademark
- An availability search in the trademark register to assess the chances of obtaining the desired registration

Only a professional in trademark registration can provide you with adequate advice. Yes, it costs more than if you make the deposit yourself. Just as it costs more to have your hair cut by a hairdresser than to do it yourself with a pair of scissors and a mirror. The advantages of working with an intellectual property specialist will quickly make you forget the inconvenience of spending a few extra dollars.

In any case, since August 3, 2019, any foreign person - natural or legal - who wishes to register a trademark in the United States must be represented by an American lawyer.

4. SOCIAL NETWORKS

The fourth level of protection concerns registration on social networks. Once again, I recommend that you maintain control over the registration of your company on social networks.

However, these generally allow for the addition of a second administrator, with varying degrees of control. In such a case, it may be wise to retain the services of an outside person or firm that specializes in managing your professional presence on social networks.

5. SEARCH ENGINES

Finally, the fifth level of protection concerns search engine registration. It is really not complicated to register your company on the various search engines. You can easily do it yourself, without the intervention of a third party. However, external help will generally be appreciated for the creation and follow-up of paid ads on these search engines.

~

Finally, here are three points you should remember.

1. WRITTEN CONTRACT

If you hire a consultant or outside firm, never rely on their verbal promises. Instead, require that your agreement be set out in a written contract, which you will have read and understood before signing. This contract must at least cover the following points:

- Nature of the services to be rendered
- Price and duration of services
- Ownership of brand names, domain names, etc.
- Control and management
- Termination of the contract

Never forget that a small pencil is better than a large memory.

2. NISSAN.COM

In 1994, Mr. Uzi Nissan registered the domain name *nissan.com* to host the website of his company Nissan Computer Corp. More than five years after this registration, the car manufacturer Nissan sued Mr. Nissan, alleging brand spoofing. For 20 years, the manufacturer tirelessly continued its proceedings against Mr. Nissan's small company, but in vain. Today, the car manufacturer uses the domain name *nissanusa.com*.

3. CAR MAT

In 1982, two Canadian friends invented a revolutionary car mat. Instead of hiring a patent agent to protect their invention, they decided to prepare their application themselves and submit it to the Canadian Intellectual Property Office. A patent was subsequently issued in their favor, thus providing their invention with legal protection and exclusive commercialization rights for 20 years.

Just two years later, a foreign company flooded Canada with a similar product. The two friends immediately sued for patent infringement. The foreign company responded with an application to cancel the patent for lack of description. Unfortunately for our two Canadian friends, the patent cancellation application was granted by the court.

The moral of this story is simple: just because you have a pair of scissors and a mirror does not mean you are a competent hairdresser.

7 - HOW TO CHANGE YOUR BUSINESS NAME

7.1 - WHY CHANGE YOUR BUSINESS NAME?

Over the course of its existence, your company may change its name. Sometimes by choice, often by obligation. Here are some reasons to change your company name.

ACQUISITION OF A BUSINESS BY ANOTHER

- Kinko's > FedEx Kinko's > FedEx Office

ADAPTATION TO A SPECIFIC MARKET

- Danone > Dannon — in the United States
- Staples > Bureau en Gros — in Québec

ADOPTION OF A PRODUCT NAME

- Research in Motion > BlackBerry
- Tokyo Telecommunications Engineering > Sony

ADOPTION OF THE NAME OF A SUBSIDIARY

- BSN > Danone
- EADS > Airbus
- Kesa Electricals > Groupe Darty
- Matsushita > Panasonic

ADDITION OF A FAMILY TOUCH

- Boulden > Boulden Brothers

NEGATIVE ASSOCIATION

- Isis Equity Partners > Livingbridge
- Isis Wallet > Softcard

CHANGE OF CORPORATE MISSION

- Weight Watchers > WW

TECHNOLOGICAL CHANGE

- Bell Cellular > Bell Mobility

DEATH OR DEPARTURE OF A PARTNER OR CO-FOUNDER

- Pigeon, Allard > Pigeon and Partners

REQUEST BY A TRADEMARK OWNER

- Shopify Ninjas > Blackbelt Commerce

GEOGRAPHICAL EXPANSION

- Manhattan Snoring and Sleep Center > Eos Sleep
- Minnesota Manufacturing and Mining > 3M

MERGER BETWEEN TWO COMPANIES

- Axa and UAP > Axa-UAP > Axa
- Sagem and Snecma > Safran
- Time Warner and AOL > AOL Time Warner

THREAT OF LEGAL ACTION

- Danone Bio > Danone Activia
- Hot Dogma > Franktuary

NAME TOO COMPLICATED TO WRITE OR PRONOUNCE

- Wysija > MailPoet

NAME TOO GENERIC

- International Business Machines > IBM
- PC's Limited > Dell

TROUBLED PAST

- Crédit lyonnais > LCL
- Genivar > WSP
- Spanghero > La Lauragaise
- United Aircraft > Pratt & Whitney

CHANGE IN SOCIAL PERCEPTION

- Gaz Metro > Energir
- TransCanada Pipelines > TC Energy

NEGATIVE FOOD REFERENCE

- Kentucky Fried Chicken > KFC

Finally, here are three points you should remember.

1. PRESSURE

Popular pressure and the threat of boycotts often force companies and organizations to consider a name change. In 2018, McGill University, located in Montreal, Canada, faced enormous public pressure to change the name of its football team from *Redmen*, which had been in place for decades. Many saw it as a pejorative reference to the people of Aboriginal origin. In April 2019, the university decided to initiate the name change process. The pressure is similar in Washington DC, where the *Redskins* are the local football team.

2. DONALD TRUMP

In 2014, Donald Trump sued two Atlantic City casinos — *Trump Plaza* and *Trump Taj Mahal* — that used his name following a duly signed contract. Trump alleged that these hotels were no longer luxurious enough to bear his name.

3. YALE UNIVERSITY

In 2017, Yale University announced that it would change the name of *Calhoun College,* one of its institutions. John C. Calhoun, a 19th century American politician and Yale graduate, was a white supremacist who considered slavery to be something positive.

7.2 - PROS AND CONS OF THE NAME CHANGE

There are several advantages, but also some disadvantages to changing your company name.

ADVANTAGES

Here are the main advantages:

- First, the name change can lead to interesting publicity, especially if the history of the name change is published on your website.
- Second, the name change can avoid significant legal costs if a third party alleges name theft or confusion.
- Third, the name change can attract new customers.
- Fourth, the name change can make it possible to obtain the desired domain name.
- Finally, changing the name can rejuvenate your company's image.

DISADVANTAGES

Now, here are some disadvantages:

- First, changing the name can involve significant costs: documentation, signs, legal fees, logo, website, bank, merchant account, etc.
- Second, changing your company name can put you and your employees under some stress before and during the name change process.
- Third, the name change may lead to a negative or mixed reaction from your current customers.

Finally, here are three points you should remember.

1. APPLE

On January 9, 2007, Apple legally changed its name from *Apple Computers Inc.* to *Apple Inc.* On the same day, at the Macworld show, Steve Jobs announced to the world the launch of the first iPhone.

2. FLORIDA

Based in Florida, the landscaping company *Wholesale Landscape Supply* — a more general than original name — commissioned Tungsten Branding to change its name. The new name *Big Earth Supply* allowed the company to increase its turnover by 200%. Its customers liked the new name so much that they ordered stickers with the new company name.

3. JOAN WEILL

Joan Weill, wife of the founder of *Citigroup*, wanted to make a $20 million donation to *Paul Smith's College*. There was only one condition: the educational institution had to change its name to *Joan Weill-Paul Smith's College*. More than 3,000 people opposed the name change through an Internet petition. Finally, a judge rejected the request for a name change and Mrs. Weill did not make the proposed donation.

7.3 - THE 4 STEPS OF THE NAME CHANGE

The process of changing your company name must be followed in a thoughtful and professional manner. In this context, it is essential to use the services of various specialists, including your lawyer and accountant. Here are four steps that should guide you through this stressful, yet exciting time.

1. CHECK

The first step is to check the availability of the chosen name at several levels:

- Business register of the state in which your company was created
- Business register of the state or states in which your company does business
- Domain names register
- Search engines
- Social networks
- Trademark Registry - in the United States and abroad

2. PLAN

The second step is to plan the actions that need to be taken. Among these actions, you must plan in particular:

- The effective date of the name change
- The information campaign around this name change

Ideally, you will appoint a person to be responsible for the planning of your company's name change. This one will be very busy for a minimum period of three to six months.

3. CHANGE

The third step is to change the name, of course at the legal level, but also at the operational level. Here is a non-exhaustive list of the elements that you must modify or have modified:

Documentation

- Account statements
- Business cards
- Envelopes
- Invoices
- Letterhead paper
- Pamphlets and brochures
- Standard contracts

Signs

- Indoor
- Outside

Registration in directories

- Associations
- Telephone

Registration on search engines

- Bing Places for Business
- Google My Business
- Yahoo! Small Business

Registration in registers

- Trademarks

Permits and licences

- Federal
- State
- County
- City
- Regulatory agencies

Company logo

Website

- Domain names
- Email addresses
- Email signatures

4. INFORM

The fourth step is to inform your professional environment of the change of your company name. Information is generally provided at two specific times:

- Before the name change: what will happen
- After the name change: what happened

Here are the people, companies, and organizations you need to inform, and often even involve at various stages of the name change:

Employees

Customers

Suppliers of goods and services

Professionals

- Accountants
- Lawyers
- Tax experts

Public utilities

- Electricity
- Gas
- Internet
- Telephone
- Water

Governmental authorities

- Internal Revenue Service — IRS
- State
- County

- City
- Regulatory bodies

Financial services providers

- Banks
- Merchant account providers (credit cards)
- PayPal

Insurance companies

- Damages
- Liability
- Life and disability

Associations to which your company belongs

Other service providers

On their website or on some social networks, several companies detail the circumstances surrounding their name change. This is a great idea, because people have always loved stories.

Finally, here are three points you should remember.

1. CHANGE

Here are some of the company name changes that are now part of history:

- Arthur Andersen > Accenture

- BackRub > Google
- Brad's Drink > Pepsi
- Sound of Music > Best Buy
- Jerry's Guide to the World Wide Web > Yahoo!

2. KINKO'S

Sometimes it can be useful to make a step-by-step name change, at least in the mind of the public. In 1970, *Kinko's* was founded by Paul Orfalea, whose nickname was *Kinko* because of his curly hair. This company offered reproduction and printing services. It quickly became popular throughout the United States.

In 2004, Fedex acquired Kinko's for $2.4 billion. In order to ease the transition in the minds of its customers, Kinko's changed its name to *FedEx Kinko's*. In 2008, the name was again changed to *FedEx Office*. Nevertheless, for years, several of the chain's stores left posters in their windows, still indicating the well-known name *Kinko's*.

3. CHRISTIANE MAYER

In 2003, a good friend of mine, Christiane Mayer, consulted me for a brainstorming session. She wanted to discuss her company *Christiane Mayer Réseau-Conseil Inc.* offering professional services in the pharmaceutical field. Her company had only been in existence for two years.

After talking with her for several hours, I persuaded her to change the name of her company: "*Christiane, in 20 or 25 years, when you are ready to retire, how are you going to sell a company with your own name? The identification of your company will be far too focused on your own person.* "

A few months after our meeting, Christiane changed her company name to *Crescendo Pharma Inc*. Today, she still congratulates herself on taking my advice.

7.4 - CHANGE YOUR DOMAIN NAME

It is possible that, during the existence of your company, you may wish to change its domain name.

REASONS

The following are the main reasons for such a decision.

1. You want to shorten your domain name:

- seomoz.org > moz.com
- askjeeves.com > ask.com
- thekarchergroup.com > tkg.com

2. You want a more user-friendly or more popular domain name:

- gogopro.us > gogopro.com

3. You want to have the short version of your domain name, in addition to its long version:

- pitneybowes.com + pb.com
- facebook.com + fb.com
- overstock.com + o.co

4. You want to change the name of your company:

- ernstandyoung.com > ey.com

5. You want to use a more targeted domain extension:

- gracetreerestaurant.com > gracetree.restaurant

PROCESS

Now, here are the main steps in the process of changing your domain name:

- You must permanently redirect all the pages of your website to the new domain name.
- Ideally, you should keep the URL structure the same.
- You must submit, if necessary, a new plan of your website - *sitemap* - in your *Google Search Console* and *Bing Webmaster Tools* customer area.
- You must create the new email addresses.
- You must redirect messages sent to old email addresses to new ones.
- You must broadcast your new domain name: website, blog, podcast, press release, etc.

Finally, here are three points you should remember.

1. SUMO.COM

The founder of the website *sumome.com* wanted to shorten his domain name. He wanted it so much that he paid $1.5 million to acquire the domain name *sumo.com*. You will find the link to his story in the *Useful Resources* section.

2. SHORTER

In most situations, you change your domain name to a shorter version. So, just like in the case of your company name, shorter is better.

3. AMAZON

Before making his final choice on *amazon.com*, Jeff Bezos used the domain name *relentless.com*. It still works and automatically redirects visitors to the Amazon website.

7.5 - CHANGE YOUR TRADEMARK

In some circumstances, your company may want to change one or more of its brands. This is not an ordinary exercise, because the strength of a trademark is its longevity. Therefore, there must be excellent reasons for replacing one trademark with another. Rebranding is a science in itself. Several elements must be considered, analyzed, and taken into account. These include, in particular:

- The perception of your customers
- The meaning of the new trademark, in its original language - if any - and in any foreign language
- The availability of the domain name
- The link between the old and new trademark
- The costs associated with rebranding

A company name is often the name of its main brand. Therefore, the change of both at the same time must be carefully planned.

Finally, here are three points you should remember.

1. HOTMAIL

On December 29, 1997, Microsoft acquired the *Hotmail* brand and website for $450 million. Renamed *MSN Hotmail*, the brand changed again to *Windows Live Hotmail*. In 2013, it finally became *Outlook*.

2. CHANGE

History contains several examples of brand change:

- Datsun > Nissan
- Il Giornale Coffee Company > Starbucks
- Peter's Super Submarines > Subway
- Confinity > PayPal
- Marufuku > Nintendo
- Software Development Labs > Oracle
- Picaboo > Snapchat

3. FOR A LONG TIME

Some company logos have been around for a long time. They have evolved over the years, but their new version often retains features of the first one. This is the case for the following companies, with the date of the appearance of their first logo:

- Deere (1876)
- Coca-Cola (1886)
- Johnson & Johnson (1886)
- Union Pacific (1888)
- Prudential (1896)
- Campbell Soup (1898)
- General Electric (1900)
- GoodYear (1901)
- Sherwin-Williams (1905)
- DuPont (1907)

8 - CONCLUSION

8.1 - THE 3 GOLDEN RULES OF YOUR BUSINESS NAME

In conclusion, here are three important rules you should remember before naming your company.

RULE NO. 1

Your company name must respect seven characteristics.

- Short
- Easy to write and spell
- Easy to pronounce
- Pleasant sound
- Pleasant visual appearance
- Easy to understand meaning
- Original - unique, memorable, and attractive

RULE NO. 2

Your company name must be available everywhere.

- Companies register
- Domain names register
- Trademarks register
- Social networks
- Search engines

RULE NO. 3

Rules 1 and 2 can sometimes be broken.

Life is littered with examples of company names, domain names, and brand names that have stood out for their unique, different, and even disturbing aspect. In the end, you are the ultimate decision maker.

Now, you have the tools that will allow you to choose your company name brilliantly.

If you enjoyed this practical guide, feel free to post a comment on the website where you got it.

If you have any questions, comments, or suggestions, please do not hesitate to contact me.

Thank you and good luck in your American adventure!

USEFUL RESOURCES

You will find the list of useful resources at:

www.corpomax.com/name

This list of useful resources is constantly updated and enriched, especially by your contributions.

If you find a site or a web page that should be in this list, please do not hesitate to send me the link.

In addition, if any of the links on this list are broken, please let me know.

Happy surfing!

ACKNOWLEDGMENTS

I would like to sincerely thank:

- My wife **Sylvie DUSSAULT ALLARD**, Director of Customer Service at CorpoMax, who always shares my creative and literary impulses - often in spite of herself
- My son **Jérémie ALLARD**, who meticulously revised the English version of the three practical guides, in addition to being the narrator in their audio version
- My stepdaughter **Véronique ALLARD**, Managing Director at CorpoMax, with whom I have had the pleasure of working for more than 10 years
- My friend **Marie-Andrée LEMIEUX**, highly talented artist, who has been taking care of my imaging and graphic design needs since 1995
- My colleague **Bettina KARPEL**, lawyer and legal translator, who has been working on my translation needs since 1995
- My friend **Christine BUREAU**, virtual collaborator and responsible for the launch of the practical guides in the *Yes to Entrepreneurs*® series

ABOUT VINCENT ALLARD

Since 1981, Vincent Allard has been a lawyer and a member of the Quebec Bar. He is also a member of the Canadian Bar Association and the American Bar Association.

He holds three university degrees:

- Law degree - LL.L. - from University of Montréal
- Master of Business Law - LL.M. - University of Ottawa, Canada
- Master of Business Administration - MBA - from École des HEC in Montreal, Canada.

For 18 years, Vincent Allard practiced business law, including corporate law and commercial litigation, primarily as a founding partner of the Pigeon, Allard law firm in Montreal.

In 1995, he co-founded Jurifax (jurifax.com), a legal publishing company that distributes more than 600 legal forms and other legal products via the Internet.

In 2001, shortly after emigrating to the United States, he founded CorpoMax (corpomax.com). Located in the state of Delaware, CorpoMax offers U.S. company formation and U.S. trademark services to thousands of entrepreneurs and professionals working in more than 50 countries.

In 2017, he launched DictoMax (dictomax.com), which offers online training to entrepreneurs and professionals.

In 2020, Vincent Allard published three practical guides for entrepreneurs:

- In English and French
- In digital, paperback, and audio formats
- All part of the *Yes to Entrepreneurs®* series.

For more than 15 years, Vincent Allard has provided training on the organization and launch of companies in the United States, mainly to foreign entrepreneurs, lawyers, accountants and tax specialists.

TO CONTACT VINCENT ALLARD

- Email: vallard@corpomax.com
- Phone: +1 302 266 8200
- Skype: corpomax

linkedin.com/in/corpomax
twitter.com/corpomax
youtube.com/corpomax
facebook.com/corpomax

BOOKS BY VINCENT ALLARD

www.corpomax.com/practical-guides

How to Start Your Business in the United States

Create Your U.S. Company

in Delaware or Elsewhere in the USA

How to Name Your Business in the United States

Find and Protect the Name of Your Company

in the United States and Abroad

How to Open Your Bank Account in the United States

Open and Manage Your

Business or Personal Account in the USA

Ces livres sont aussi disponibles en français :

www.corpomax.com/guides-pratiques

LEGAL INFORMATION

This practical guide contains a lot of information available on the Internet from public sources. However, it is by no means a legal, accounting or tax guide. Therefore, you should be well aware that this guide does not provide legal, accounting or tax advice. To obtain such advice, tailored to your particular situation, you must therefore contact a lawyer, accountant or tax expert working in the appropriate jurisdiction.

Every effort has been made to make this guide as complete and accurate as possible. Although the author and the publisher have prepared this guide with the greatest of care, and have made every effort to ensure the accuracy, they assume no responsibility or liability for errors, inaccuracies, or omissions. Before you begin, check with the appropriate authorities to ensure compliance with all laws and regulations.

On the other hand, this guide may contain mistakes in typography or content. Also, this guide contains information valid only until the date of its publication.

Therefore, this practical guide should be used as a guide only - not as the ultimate source of information. The purpose of this guide is for educational purposes only. The author and the publisher do not warrant that the information contained in this guide is fully complete and shall not be responsible for any errors or omissions. The author and the publisher shall have neither liability nor responsibility to any person or entity with respect to any loss or damage caused or alleged to be caused directly or indirectly by this guide, nor do they make any claims or promises of your ability to generate income by using any of the information contained in this guide.

Finally, the list of useful resources, which is offered as a bonus with this guide, contains a series of hyperlinks, which are provided for informational purposes only. The author and the publisher do not guarantee that the information contained in the websites concerned by these hyperlinks is complete, adequate or truthful. Therefore, the author and the publisher incur no liability to any person or entity for any loss or damage caused or suspected to be caused directly or indirectly by the use of the information contained in one or more of the websites concerned. The author and publisher make no representation or promise of your ability to generate income by using the information contained in one or more of the relevant websites.

Made in the USA
Monee, IL
04 November 2026

67385791R00184